LIVING
AND
DYING
WHILE
BLACK
IN
AMERICA

THE
BEAST
SIDE

D. WATKINS

10644735

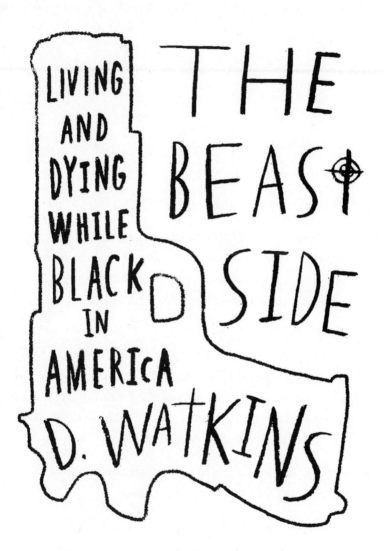

LIVING AND DYING WHILE BLACK IN AMERICA

THE BEAST SIDE

D. WATKINS

FOREWORD BY DAVID TALBOT

Hot Books

Copyright © 2015 by D. Watkins

Paperback Copyright © 2016 by D. Watkins

All rights reserved. No part of this book may be reproduced in any manner without the express written consent of the publisher, except in the case of brief excerpts in critical reviews or articles. All inquiries should be addressed to Hot Books, 307 West 36th Street, 11th Floor, New York, NY 10018.

Hot Books books may be purchased in bulk at special discounts for sales promotion, corporate gifts, fund-raising, or educational purposes. Special editions can also be created to specifications. For details, contact the Special Sales Department, Skyhorse Publishing, 307 West 36th Street, 11th Floor, New York, NY 10018 or info@skyhorsepublishing.com.

Hot Books® and Skyhorse Publishing® are registered trademarks of Skyhorse Publishing, Inc.®, a Delaware corporation.

Visit our website at www.skyhorsepublishing.com.

10 9 8 7 6 5 4 3 2

Library of Congress Cataloging-in-Publication Data is available on file.

Cover design by Na Kim
ISBN: 978-1-5107-1639-1
Ebook ISBN: 978-1-5107-1640-7

Printed in the United States of America

To Freddie Gray, and all the other innocent victims of senseless violence.

We won't let you die in vain.

Genius Child

This is a song for the genius child.

Sing it softly, for the song is wild.

Sing it softly as ever you can—

Lest the song get out of hand.

Nobody loves a genius child.

Can you love an eagle, Tame or wild?

Can you love an eagle, Wild or tame?

Can you love a monster

Of frightening name?

Nobody loves a genius child.

Kill him—and let his soul run wild.

—Langston Hughes

I love America more than any other country in this world, and, exactly for this reason, I insist on the right to criticize her perpetually.

—James A. Baldwin

The Beast Side Playlist

Foreword

Oh Baltimore, man it's hard just to live, just to live . . .

White Americans who pride themselves on being racially tuned in—and yes, that would include me—liked to think we turned a major corner back in 2008 with the election of Barack Obama, a 21st century emancipation of sorts that we then proceeded to ratify in 2012. And no matter what has happened since then, America will always have that ecstatic victory night when the president-elect and his family strode onstage at Chicago's Grant Park and it seemed, for that moment, we were all living the dream together. Then reality set in—a reality that seemed to grow more grim with each police killing of an unarmed African American citizen or some other explosion of racial violence.

We watched with growing horror as innocent black lives were brutally extinguished in New York and Florida and Ferguson and Baltimore and Charleston and Cleveland and Los Angeles. And even here in San Francisco, which still likes to pride itself as a progressive outpost, we were not immune. We watched on our laptops and smart phones as a young, slight man named Mario Woods was put up against a wall by a firing squad of police officers and summarily executed. The SFPD violence against black and brown men continued, until growing community pressure—capped by a hunger strike led by protestors known as the Frisco Five—finally brought down the police chief. But just as progress seems to being made, here in San Francisco and elsewhere, there is suddenly another stunning video of wanton police violence.

And so we had—in back-to-back succession—Baton Rouge and the Minneapolis suburb where Philando Castile was murdered in cold blood, while his fiancée captured his final, heartbreaking minutes on video. And then, inevitably, we had Dallas, where five police officers lost their lives amid the growing rage of millions of Americans who feel abandoned by the justice system. *No justice, no peace.* The chant grows increasingly ominous.

White America can no longer deny the stark truth that black Americans have known all their lives. If you are black, you are marked. You are stopped by police, arrested, prosecuted, jailed— and yes, killed by men with badges—at rates that are shockingly higher than those for other Americans. And when police officers take another innocent life, they inevitably go unpunished. When you put on a police uniform in America, you are granted a license to kill, if your victims are black, brown or poor.

Of course, as D. Watkins sharply observes here, African Americans are marked in other ways too. They continue to be the canaries in our coalmine—the citizens whose unequal opportunities and unequal rights reveal a deeper truth about the fundamental sins of our nation. Black families in the inner city bear the brunt of economic malaise, collapsing urban infrastructure, deteriorating schools, and police violence. But the rot is spreading. Today, the east side of Baltimore and Oakland, tomorrow the suburbs.

The nation's schools, playgrounds, offices and shopping malls still remain surprisingly segregated. We live in our own worlds. The more fortunate like to think crime and misery is carefully contained, that it happens to others. The fire might seem a long way off, but most of us can smell the smoke. Many of us are just one payday, just one twist of bad luck from the inferno. The rich are getting richer and everyone else is getting screwed; the 99 percent are all in this together.

If African Americans have historically been America's sacrificial victims, they have also been its prophets and crusaders. When I was young, it was prophetic black leaders who tried to awaken the country before it was too late. And it was books like James Baldwin's *The Fire Next Time* and George Jackson's *Soledad Brother*. These were the writers who had looked into the fire. They had much to tell us about what they saw there, if we were smart enough and brave enough to listen.

Now we have D. Watkins and *The Beast Side: Living (and Dying) While Black in America*. Watkins is a native son of Baltimore's east side--the beast side. He has survived the kind of life in urban America that has claimed the lives of many of his friends, family members, schoolmates and brothers and sisters on the corner—so many, in fact, that he compares his life to war, because that's what it is. He writes with the compassion, and unsentimental clarity, of a survivor—of a man who is passionately determined to stop the cycles of violence and suffering that have long been inflicted on his community from within and without. Watkins's voice is strong and original. He cuts through all the media windbaggery, political grandstanding and preachy banality that define America's racial debate these days.

The Beast Side is a rare, highly personal dispatch from the streets. At times it's a roar to fight the power, or a lament to the heavens about the tragedies that seem to have no end. At other times, it's an urgent plea to the young ones in his care to act smart and stay alive, or it's straight talk for a community in need of radical self-transformation. This is the first book to capture our post-Obama reality in all its maddening, and occasionally inspiring, complexity. It must be read by Americans of all colors and all social backgrounds—by anyone who bleeds for our country and prays for its deliverance.

The Beast Side signaled the birth of Hot Books, a new imprint that I'm overseeing in partnership with Skyhorse Publishing. The Hot Books series features powerfully concise books on the most burning issues of our day. Some Hot Books, like *The Beast Side,* take the form of argument and storytelling. Others are works of investigative journalism, trying to fill the void left by too many newspapers and magazines in the digital age, when in-depth reporting and editorial budgets have been severely cut back. Whether they are presenting searing essay collections or works of crusading journalism, Hot Books authors like D. Watkins draw inspiration from that great prophetic tradition of speaking truth to power.

Join us as we seek to rekindle the fading embers of our democracy, by spreading the word about Hot Books to your book clubs, schools, universities, local bookstores, libraries and social media forums. It's time to speak the unspeakable, and think the unthinkable. Welcome to Hot Books.

—David Talbot
September 2016

Introduction

One night, I participated in a peaceful protest near downtown Baltimore. My fellow protestors and I were standing in solidarity with the citizens of Ferguson, Missouri, over the murder of Mike Brown—an innocent African American teen, who was on his way to college when he was cut down by a policeman's bullets. It felt good to unite with so many different people for the same cause—a diverse group with handmade signs and a shared sense of outrage. But even as we shouted for justice, I knew it wasn't enough from my experiences in rallying for the Jena six and Trayvon Martin. I do have an immense amount of respect for protestors, marchers, and organizers—but in the end, after all that chanting, marching, and lying down in traffic, Darren Wilson, the cop who murdered Brown, still went free, and cops in America still feel comfortable killing innocent black people.

Every time a black body falls at the hands of a rogue cop, the same protests erupt on one side, and the same naive voices echo the same nonsense on the other: "Well, if they were innocent, why did they run? Why did they attack an officer, why didn't they obey?" I get where these confused voices come from. In a perfect world, innocent people should not *have* to run or protect themselves from the people responsible for protecting us. However, America is far from perfect, and African Americans are about as safe as a chunk of steak in a den full of starving lions. It *doesn't matter if you stay or fight back or run*, because either way they'll murder you.

Freddie Gray in Baltimore ran, and when they caught him, he was murdered.

Walter Scott in South Carolina ran, and he was murdered, too.

Oscar Grant in Oakland was face down on the ground with the cuffs on, and they murdered him.

John Crawford in Dayton was minding his own business, shopping at Wal-Mart, holding one of the store's BB guns and an officer opened fire within seconds of interacting with him.

Mike Brown in Ferguson, who we were rallying for that day in Baltimore, put his hands up, and the cops blew holes through them.

Sean Bell in New York was just trying to get married, and police killed him.

Eric Garner in Staten Island pleaded for his life after he was in custody—on video, in public, broad daylight—and they still killed him.

Ervin Edwards—mentally ill and partially deaf—had his pants hanging low, so police tasered him to death after he was in custody.

Jonathan Ferrell in North Carolina wanted some help because he was in a car accident; cops shot him to death as he reached out to them for assistance.

Tamir Rice in Cleveland was only 12. Being a kid can't save you, because he was gunned down, too.

Thaddeus McCarroll in St. Louis was killed because he had a knife and a Bible.

Rekia Boyd in Chicago was killed by an off-duty cop who fired into a dark alley.

Ramarley Graham in New York tried to run into his home, and they got him.

Kathryn Johnston, a 92-year-old woman in Atlanta, was relaxing in her home, and police stampeded in like cowboys and killed her in a botched drug raid.

Akai Gurley in Brooklyn just happened to be in his stairwell minding his own business—with no weapon—and was killed for that. Just like they hearlessly murdered Sandra Bland and Alton Sterling and Philando Castile.

You can be from Africa like Amadou Diallo in New York or known as a nice guy around Baltimore like Tyrone West or Anthony Anderson: It doesn't matter, no black person is safe. Kids, grannies, city workers, hustlers, church boys, prom queens, junkies, whatever—they'll murder you.

These killings happen almost every day in America, so much that the newspapers should print a daily death count, with photos of the casualties, like they do during wartime—because for black America, this *is* wartime. What's disgusting is that nearly all of the officers who commit these heinous acts are found innocent. Many aren't even charged due to the various versions of the "Law Enforcement Officers' Bill of Rights" that exist in every state. In Maryland, where I live, police officers get ten days before they even have to speak about the killings they're involved in, giving them ample time to assemble the mountains of lies that normally get them off. *The Guardian* recently reported that police will kill blacks this year at twice the rate of whites, and this is the norm.

If some racist cop isn't gunning us down, then a racist psycho is trying to do the same. And just like in the police cases, white privilege prevails—even in outrageous incidents like the massacre at Charleston's Emanuel AME Church.

Check the manner in which the cops apprehended Dylann Storm Roof, the murderer and domestic terrorist whom the media did a great job of *not* calling a domestic terrorist, because of white privilege.

At the time of his arrest, Roof was an armed and dangerous fugitive, who had heartlessly gunned down nine church members. But he still received the utmost care when he was taken into police custody. The cops even bought him a hamburger and fries at a nearby Burger King when he told them he was hungry. Later they gave him a nice bulletproof vest to ensure that he wouldn't receive any harm as he was gently escorted to and from the courthouse. When the cameras flashed, he was clean and spotless, with every hair of his Lloyd from *Dumb and Dumber* cut in place.

Imagine how the cops would have reacted if a hate-spewing, black extremist had shot up a white church prayer meeting, telling his victims as he blasted them at point-blank range, "I'll give you something to pray about." Let's just say he wouldn't have been treated to a Whopper. If he were black, he probably would have ended up like the innocent and unarmed Cleveland couple, Timothy Russell and Malissa Williams, who also fled the police but received no empathy restraint, or burgers when they were apprehended—just 137 bullets sprayed into their car for being on the wrong side of privilege. There's a collection of contemporary cases that display similar results.

Talking about white privilege and its role in these shootings always makes white people uneasy—probably because no one wants to feel like they have an unfair advantage over another person solely based on skin color. However, if you are white in America, you have an unfair advantage solely based on skin color. So deal with it. You'll probably go to a better school, have a more high-paying job, live in a safer neighborhood, never be profiled by police officers, get lower interest rates, and always have the luxury of walking around stores in peace. It is that way, it has been that way and chances are, it will remain that way for the foreseeable future. Dr. Karl Alexander of Johns Hopkins University recently completed 35 years of research dealing with the poor white experience vs. the poor black experience. He published his findings in his book *The Long Shadow*, observing that whites use more drugs but are less likely to be charged with a crime. In Baltimore—where 97 percent of the black people who are born in poverty die in poverty—it's easier for a white person with some jail time on their record to get a job than a black person with some college.

Like many, I'm sick and tired of the same old, same old when it comes to the inequality of justice in America. I'm tired of officers getting away with murder, and even though I value all of the protestors and street organizers, the stream of outrageous verdicts in police shooting cases finally made me realize that marching is not the best way for me create the change I'd like to see.

As a result, I decided to shift my mission toward literacy, broadly defined. Poverty, injustice, and reading comprehension issues go hand in hand, like white cops and innocent verdicts. On the other side of the spectrum, I believe that the officers who commit these crimes are semi-literate as well—especially in terms of understanding the world of those they interact with on the streets of Baltimore, Ferguson, and many other urban places around the country. That leaves us with two groups who can't communicate, so they clash and it ends in death.

Putting out *The Beast Side* is my first contribution toward combating this national crisis. Telling our stories and educating people are the best things we can do, if we hope to pull ourselves out of this bloody mess. My goal is to write stories that get nontraditional readers excited about reading—as reading saved me.

Before I became a reader, I had no problem breaking a Hennessy bottle across the back of some guy's head. That type of anger in me was solely attributed to an inability to communicate. It's the same anger that many officers carry inside them when they patrol the streets—and it's identical to the rage that burns in the poorest parts of cities. Reading has given me the ability to channel that anger into strategic, solution-based thinking, the kind of thinking that will be key in fixing our cities. I also want to encourage more young and poor minorities to write and raise as much awareness as possible about the ills we all face.

The Beast Side also recognizes that killer white cops aren't the only ones plaguing the black community. Black cops kill us, too. We kill ourselves through violence and by the food we consume from the poisonous restaurants that surround our neighborhoods in addition to some of the food we cook for ourselves. And then there's the major health-care disparities between blacks and whites, our troubled schools, our poor living conditions, and the many racist policies our system has in place (e.g., the War on Drugs and our ever-growing prison-industrial complex). *The Beast Side* tries to shed light on all of the factors that negatively affect our communities and the many ways that society tries to bury us—not realizing that we are seeds, growing into the change that has been forcing our nation to reform. I was once a part of this vicious cycle in many capacities, so I have some valuable insight to share on coping mechanisms, what's needed in our neighborhoods, and some of the things that saved many of the people I grew up with.

I hope *The Beast Side* will do the same for many, by exposing these problems, sparking a national dialogue for change, challenging our elected officials and inspiring others to look deeper and to fight the underlying, systemic ills responsible for our pain.

SIDE ONE

Stoop Stories

So last week, I'm posted up, sharing a sandwich and a cigarette with a friend in one of the most dangerous neighborhoods in America, and my phone buzzes. On the other end is one of my old professors asking me to tell one of my wild childhood stories at the Stoop Storytelling Series, a live show at Center Stage in downtown Baltimore.

A stoop show, I thought: kind of like what I do on the corner in my own neighborhood every day. I'm always surrounded by stoops, Baltimore stoops made of cracked and chipped marble steps where all we do is tell street stories: who's getting money, who's going to jail, who murdered who, whose album is hot, who is that girl, who's driving what, and who's coming home from jail.

This would be easy, the same thing, but in someone else's neighborhood. I agreed to it like I agreed to the last fifteen opportunities that fell in my lap. I'd recently written "Too Poor for Pop Culture," an essay for *Salon* that went viral and made me semi-relevant on the Internet and the man to know on the local scene. My next goal was to sign a book deal; I'd learned that exposure and platform are key, so I looked forward to the event.

The day of the show rolled around, and I was backstage with my fellow cast members and storytellers. These guys were Easter-sharp, with starched button-ups and wingtips; the women matched them in pumps and flashy adult versions of their prom dresses.

Obviously, I missed the dress code memo because I walked in wearing a black hoodie and some black Air Jordans. But no one really cared about my outfit—they greeted me with gifts, praise, and love when I arrived backstage.

One of the organizers hit me with some drink tickets so I could get a little buzz before the show. I grabbed them and blasted into the lobby to redeem them. That's when I realized. This is one of *those events*.

By "those events" I mean a segregated Baltimore show that blacks don't even know about. I walked through a universe of white faces, and I wondered, how is this even possible? How could we be in the middle of Baltimore, a predominately black city where African Americans make up more than 60 percent of the population, at a sold-out event, with no black people—except for me and the friends I brought?

I swallowed my drink and grabbed another for the stage. The hostess gave me an amazing intro and welcomed me to the mic. I walked up and said, "This ain't the stoop I'm used to. There's no pit bulls, red cups, or blue flashing lights, but I'll make it work!" I paused, took a look at the crowd, and honestly felt like I wasn't in Baltimore.

My black friends call it Baldamore, Harm City, or Bodymore, Murderland. My white friends call it Balti-mo, Charm City, or Smalltimore while falling head over heels in love with the quaint pubs, trendy cafés, and distinctive little shops. I just call it home.

We all love Baltimore, Maryland. It's one of those places that people never leave—literally. I know people, blacks and whites, who have been residents for thirty-plus years and haven't even been as far north as Philly or as far south as DC.

Baltimore is one of the few major metropolitan cities with a small-town feel, and it has an extremely colorful history. The Town of Baltimore was founded in 1729 and named after the Englishman Cecilius Calvert, better known as Lord Baltimore. In the years that followed, Germans and Scots settled the cheap land, which was too poor for the tobacco farming that made the southern part of state so rich but was good enough for wheat. Proximity to water helped Baltimore flourish, with a thriving ship market at Fell's Point, now a hip waterfront area with shops, coffee bars, and pubs. As Baltimore grew, flour mills, bakeries, blacksmiths, and other small, family-owned shops prospered, too.

Eventually, Baltimore took off in a major way, and as industry grew, so did the need for slaves. By 1810, Baltimore had 4,672 slaves, mostly hired out by cash-strapped owners from upper Maryland. In the heyday of the antebellum South, before the Civil War, some of those Baltimore slaves made enough money on the side to buy their own freedom and eventually the freedom of their families and friends.

Maryland sided with the Union during the Civil War by not declaring secession, even though it was a slave state—though some people in southern Maryland joined the Confederates anyway to keep their slaves and their tobacco farms. Some Confederate supporters attacked Union soldiers, causing twelve deaths and sparking the Baltimore riot of 1861. After that, the Union Army had to step in and occupy Baltimore until 1865.

Is this how the two Baltimores began? As a place split on ide-
ologies because it was too south to be North and too north to be
South—was this the start?

It is now 149 years later, and nothing has changed. I went to all-
black schools, lived in an all-black neighborhood, and had almost no
interactions with whites other than teachers and housing police until
college, where I got my first introduction to the other Baltimore.

My SAT scores and high school grades were exceptional for an
east Baltimore kid, especially because a large number of the males in
my area didn't even consider college. This gained me acceptance into
schools that probably wouldn't have admitted me if I weren't a ghetto
kid. Thirsty for a new experience, I wanted to go to an out-of-state college. But my plans were derailed when, months before my high school
graduation in 2000, my brother Bip and my close friend DI were murdered. I became severely depressed and rejected the idea of school.

Most of my family and friends came around in an effort to get
me back on track. My best friend, Hurk, hit my crib every day.

I met Hurk way back in the 1990s. His mom sucked dick for
crack until she became too hideous to touch. Her gums were bare,
her skin peeled like dried glue, chap lived on her lips, and she always
smelled like trash-juice. Then she caught AIDS and died.

Hurk's my age. His family was a billion dollars below the poverty line. He had so many holes in his shoes that his feet were bruised.
I started giving him clothes that I didn't want, and he stayed with us
most nights. We became brothers.

At thirteen, Hurk started hustling drugs for Bip and never
looked back. He loved his job. Hurk was organized, he recruited, and
he out-worked everyone else on the corner. Like a little Bip, Hurk

beat the sun to work every morning: 4 a.m. every day in the blister-
ing cold, with a fist full of loose vials. He never fucked up Bip's count
and seized every advancement opportunity. His workload tripled
after Bip passed, but he called every day.

"D, how you holdin' up, shorty?" said Hurk.

"I don't even know. Man, I been in this house for weeks," I
replied.

"Naw, nigga, get out. Get a cut, nigga, go do some shit! Least
you still alive!"

"You right," I said as I sat on the edge of my bed. My eyes swelled
like a prizefighter fifteen rounds in. "Wet floor" signs were needed
for my tears.

"What the fuck, yo, you cry every day?" Hurk said.

"Naw, well no, shit. I dunno."

"Yo anyway, I'm gonna murder dat nigga that popped Bip.
Ricky Black, bitch ass. So go live, nigga, get some new clothes, pussy,
or sumthin.'"

I picked my head up for the first time in days. I didn't know
my brother even had static with Ricky Black—or if Ricky actually
killed him. They played ball together a week before Bip died. But it
didn't matter if Hurk killed Ricky, or I did, because someone would
eventually.

Murder made Hurk smile theatrically; he leaped from his seat.
"Nigga, I keep the ratchet on me," he said, lifting his sweatshirt to
show me the gun gleaming on his waist.

I told him he was crazy, but I didn't care. I wouldn't commit that
murder—I'm not a killer. Or am I? I am capable of hate, and I am a
direct product of this culture of retaliation—a culture that won't let
me sleep, eat, or rest until I know that Bip's killer is dead.

"Be careful," I said.

"You should think about school, D," said Hurk on his way out the door. "Bip would like that. Plus, I won't be around too much, yo. I'm on the run for some bullshit. Dem boyz kicked my crib in—shit!"

He was right. My brother always wanted me to attend college: I owed Bip that.

I decided to stay in state to be close to family, so I attended Loyola University, a local school on the edge of the city.

I always thought college would be like that TV show, *A Different World*. Dimed-out Whitley Gilberts and Denise Huxtables hanging by my dorm—young, pure, and making a difference. I'd be in Jordans and Jordan jerseys or Cosby sweaters like Ron Johnson and Dwayne Wayne, getting As and living that black intellectual life on a beautiful campus. No row homes, hood-rats, housing police, or gunshots: just pizza, good girls, and opportunity. I could even graduate and be The Dude Who Saves the Hood!

A plethora of white and Asian faces smirked at me as I walked across campus the first day. This was a different world but not the world I was looking for.

There were some other black dudes there, but they weren't black like me. They spoke proper English; wore pastel-colored sweaters, Dockers chinos, and boat shoes; carried credit cards; chased Ugg-booted white girls; played sports other than basketball; and talked about "Degrassi"—*what the fuck is Degrassi?*

I wore six braids straight back like the basketball player Allen Iverson, real Gucci sweat suits, and a $15,000 mixture of mine and

Bip's old jewelry. The other students looked at me like I was an alien. I'd walk up to a student and clearly say, "Excuse me, where is the bookstore?" And he or she would look back with a twisted face, like, "I don't understand you. What are you saying?" And I had this dance with multiple students every day until I mastered my Carlton from *The Fresh Prince of Bel-Air* voice.

I related to no one, so I talked my friend Nick, who dropped out of middle school, into hanging around campus with me.

"Yo D, if any of these people act dumb, even da principal, tell me. Swear to God, I'll fuck 'em up for you, yo."

"Colleges have deans, Nick, not principals, but I guarantee I won't have any problems here."

I laughed as we sat in Nick's Camry. His face was stone. I cracked the door, split a blunt down the center with my ring finger, and dumped its guts on the sidewalk. We'd sit a block away from the school and burn two Ls of dro mixed with hash, and then it was school time.

Clean and high, I'd float through Loyola. Some of the students were racist—but not to my face—and it seemed like my professors made sure I knew I was the only black person from low-income housing on their planet. My philosophy teacher, a tweed-coat dickhead named Dr. Rose or Dr. Ross, was the worst. One time he asked, "What sport did you play to get into here?" I fantasized about having Nick pistol-whip him, but he was only a pedestrian on my road to bigger goals.

I tried to adjust to the campus culture by attending basketball games and buying a gray Loyola hoodie; I bought Nick a black one. Together we sat, emotionless, through home games—underwhelmed by the basic style of play and unaffected by the school spirit that shook the gym. Loyola students got excited over made free throws and baseline jump shots. Hood dudes like us needed thrills—rim-breaking dunks, spin moves, shit talking, finger pointing, and ankle-breaking crossovers.

Eventually, I met some cool white boys to smoke weed with. Tyler stuck out the most. He was a freshman like me but already had a hold on the campus. Girls giggled when he spoke, and most of the other freshmen lived and died for his approval. I saw him around a few times, but initially we met in the athletics center. I was shooting jumpers, and Nick was rebounding for me. Tyler walked up and said, "Nice shot. You guys gamble?"

"Shoot his head off, D! Shoot his head off, D!" chanted Nick. Tyler and I went $5 a shot for an hour or so, and I think he beat me out of $200 or $300. I paid him, and he gave me $100 back.

"What's this for?" I said, rejecting the money. He explained that he had gambled with black guys before, and he noticed that the winners always give the losers a little something back. Then he said, "Besides, you guys smell like Jamaicans! Can I get some of that?" The three of us walked back to Nick's Camry and smoked some joints. Tyler thought the bud was decent; Nick and I always had it, so we exchanged numbers and ended up building a relationship.

Sometimes we smoked and talked shit to girls together or beat the shit out of the squares that hung around in the athletics center at basketball. Tyler even took me to his crib in Bolton Hill, with beautiful brownstones that ranged from $300K well into the millions.

I really liked Tyler, but most of his friends were hard to take. They'd invite Nick and me to campus parties. We'd walk in, and the mood would change. They'd reference Dr. King and then Dr. Dre, and call us bro and brotha, and give us too many handshakes. They tried to imitate us so we felt more comfortable, but it just felt conde-scending. The good part is that we never got into any fights and the N-word never slipped out. These parties got old to us really quick, so we stopped going.

Doing homework and adjusting to this new world helped me deal with my losses a little, but I still had sleepless nights when I would sit in the park until the sun woke me, wondering why I was alive and my brother wasn't, why Nick couldn't study and be a stu-dent too, why I was losing so many friends, and why I never got a chance to tell these people what they meant to me.

By mid-semester, I was sick of school. The work wasn't hard, but it was as boring as that show *M*A*S*H*, and trying to assimilate had become exhausting.

What would my brother say if he saw me hanging around this campus with Zack Morris and AC Slater, laughing at jokes I hated, listening to stories that bored me, going to wack basketball games, slowly conforming—being a good Negro. Referencing *Degrassi!*

I knew my brother didn't want me in the streets, but I knew he didn't want this—we were raised by Biggie, Spike Lee, 2Pac, NWA, and Public Enemy, not this Wayne Brady shit. So I said fuck it and stopped going. I had some money put up. Roughly $70,000 left behind in my brother's stash. I took that along with some cocaine he left in his safe and dove right into the family business as a full-time crack, heroin, and coke dealer.

Tyler hit me on the phone a month or so after I stopped show-ing up and said, "D, what the fuck, man? You're just not going to come back?"

He needed some weed, so I invited him down to my neigh-borhood. He had lived in Bolton Hill and Roland Park all his life, and my Baltimore blew his mind. He knew some black guys but had never really kicked in a housing project.

Tyler leaned against the gate and saw a bunch of Baptist churches, dirty little Korean stores with thirty teenage dope-dealers clogging the doors and the corner. Singing-and-dancing-and-dying dope fiends wandering around and bumping into each other like the *Thriller* zombies. Thirty-year-old pregnant grandmas. Dudes in Nikes waving automatic weapons. Unsupervised children, some barefoot and trying not to step on glass like we're in a third-world country. And us: me and my crew.

I showed him how our operation worked and who played what roles, how we changed shifts, different ways we incentivized hard work, and our methods for staying out of prison. He was infatuated to say the least.

Shortly after, Tyler discovered a void in the raw coke market throughout the Loyola and Johns Hopkins/Charles Village area, and he wanted to join our operation. I set him up with coke, and we never looked back. Tyler moved more coke in a week than most of my street people could move in a month. He built a huge clientele consisting of everyone from students to professors. We were all making crazy money, and that's how I really discovered the other Baltimore.

Black Baltimore is all about Grey Goose vodka, Hennessey cognac, crack sales, making money and running to the outskirts of the city, playing basketball, paying $40 to get into parties with $15 drinks, cook-outs, corner stores, being harassed by cops, pit bulls, dirt bikes, church, diabetes, and staying in black areas.

White Baltimore, which in most cases is only two miles away from these black areas, is all about Ketel One or Stoli vodka, Jack Daniel's whiskey and Coke, sniffing coke, Labradors, eating outside, free entrance into clubs where you buy one drink and get another free, barbeques, free-range chickens, playing Frisbee, jogging, being loved by cops, and staying in white areas.

For years, Tyler and I worked the whitest areas in the city—Fell's Point, Canton, and Federal Hill. I even stacked enough cash to move out of the hood into a Bolton Hill brownstone similar to the one Tyler's parents owned. When I told the homeboys where I lived, they thought it was more than a hundred miles away, but it was only five miles from where I hung every day.

Living in Bolton Hill taught me a lot about our city and the role that segregation plays. I liked to bring ten or fifteen of my boys from my old neighborhood up to my place to show them a little experiment that I figured out. I'd wait to around midnight and take a large, full trash bag out to the front of my house, cut it open and dump its contents all over the street. Then we'd smoke, drink, club, or whatever, but by 2 or 3 a.m., all of the trash would be gone. The city would come through and pick up everything, leaving the front of my house squeaky clean.

Then I'd do the same thing with a bag of trash in the black neighborhood closest to Bolton Hill, called Marble Hill. And the trash would sit. It would sit for days, unless residents cleaned it up. Marble Hill was known for being more dangerous, but Bolton Hill had more cops patrolling, in addition to better-kept parks and first priority when it came to snow removal.

During those years that I lived in Bolton Hill, I also hung with Nick on a corner in the hood. Different sets of crews would come and go; some died off or went to prison, but Nick maintained until 2004, when he asked me to put $60K of my own money with $100K of his and another guy's cash into this big deal that could get us ten bricks of cocaine and set us straight for life. I couldn't afford it, and I didn't want to do it. I was thinking enough was enough around the time he was thinking expansion. I was sick of funerals, wasting days on corners, and wondering when the cops would finally bag me or when it would be my turn to die.

I kept selling the little bit of drugs I had tucked away while Nick raised his money through an old-school approach. He hit every block from east to west, shaking down dealers, jamming his gun down throats, and emptying the pockets of anyone selling anything. I heard he even hung a kid named Tevin out of a window for $300: any- and everything to raise that money.

We have a saying in east Baltimore that goes, "Stick-up kids don't last long"—and it's right. Some guys from one of the many crews Nick robbed caught up with him and blew his brains out on Ashland Avenue, steps away from his grandma's house. I got the news while visiting family in LA, and that was the beginning of the end for me.

Eventually, I lost contact with Tyler, lost the house in Bolton Hill, and ended up back in the hood where I started out. I decided to go back to school in hopes of finding a job and getting a better life.

This time, I attended the University of Baltimore, which is a semi-mixed school. UB ended up being a better fit for me than Loyola. It wasn't *A Different World*, they had few black professors, and the white students at UB knew nothing about the Baltimore I'm from. But it was a mix of working people who wanted to better themselves through education, and I connected with them because of all the game I learned from Tyler.

UB is a commuter school in the heart of midtown, and you'd be surprised to see such a small number of black students and professors at a school in the middle of Baltimore. But it's true, the segregation continues. It's evident in every classroom—the blacks sit with blacks, and the whites sit with whites. We'd work together on class assignments and presentations, and then, when we would go celebrate, the whites would go to their bar, and we would celebrate at ours.

My experience at Johns Hopkins, where I finished my master of science in education, felt more extreme. I walked through the hallway on my first day in 2010, and a woman looked me up and down, stopped me, and said, "Excuse me, sir. Someone threw up in the women's bathroom. Can you handle that? Thank you."

I knew what she thought. I'm a black man at a white school, meaning I'm a janitor. I looked her in the eyes and said, "I believe in humanity," before walking away. The rest of my experience at Hopkins was just like that, but I must admit being there helped me master what I already thought I knew about the other side of Baltimore.

Simple communication, which I perfected at Hopkins, was the key. Underneath it all, I found, the privileged whites and Asians at Hopkins were the same as the black dudes in my neighborhood. We all wanted love, success, purpose, and opportunity. We are all gunning for the same things but taking different roads and using different languages along the way. Learning how to communicate with people so far removed from my reality made me smarter, and now I'm an expert. I can communicate in the roughest housing projects because of my origin and in the whitest neighborhoods because of my college experience and my time with Tyler selling good coke, and now I'm doing an event like the Stoop.

The crowd at the Stoop Storytelling Session must have been drunk: They laughed at everything I said to point where I'm considering a career as a stand-up. "Oh yeah, and black people! There are no black people on this stoop! I'm not sure if you guys noticed or not!" It was the last joke I gave before I dove into a story about me at twelve being robbed at gunpoint for my dirt bike.

My family didn't panic or call the cops—they strapped up with guns, found the dudes who robbed me, beat them down, and retrieved my bike. And even though we illegally took back my stolen bike, the overarching theme of family looking out for family connected us all. The audience at the Stoop got my perspective and had a unique chance to be invited to my side of Baltimore. It was all relatable, and the two Baltimores felt like one, but only for that night. Because after the show, I traveled back to my Baltimore, and they returned to theirs.

And even though I can easily walk through the two versions of my city, I'm still most comfortable in my origin. I'm not sure why we don't mix, but I am sure that we never will.

Lessons of a Former Dope Dealer

My grandma worked her ass off. Her worn, plump, diabetic hands scrubbed crud off chipped dishes in her kitchen minutes after she finished a ten-hour shift. She washed clothes, took care of her husband, did unpaid church work, and cooked for seventeen of my cousins and me at times. I don't remember her taking a day off. She was a hardworking homeowner in the inner city who clocked in every day until she died.

And even though she prayed for me daily in the midst of her many tasks, I still ended up on the corner like most of the men in my family. I didn't adapt to her religion, but I did inherit her work ethic.

At eighteen, I'd often slice the tips of my fingers up while shaving marble-size pieces of crack into smaller bits before shoving them into long glass vials that I rocked off for $6 a pop. I'd suck the blood off my fingers, rubber band the vials into a bundle, tuck them in my sock, and then go off to my block around 8:30 a.m. to set up shop for my ten- to twelve-hour shift.

My homie, Lil Duncan with the chubby face, who was about four years younger, would normally be shutting down and on his way to school when I started my shift. He sold heroin and normally started around 4 a.m. (you gotta beat the sunrise to slang heroin) and then closed in time to drop his little sister off at school and make his first-period class.

On any random night, midway through my shift or around the time Lil Duncan was reopening his, you could catch us on our east Baltimore corner, along with the rest of our enterprising circle, including a forty-plus loudmouth, a bunch of Niked-up teens, and some early twenty–somethings. Crackhead Lenny and his wife Loraine would most likely be in the center, beating the shit out of each other like gladiators.

"Left hook, Loraine! Left hook, Loraine!" some kids would yell as she'd belt Lenny into a three-point stance or flat on his ass. Loraine liked to step back, Ali-style, and dance a little while waiting for Lenny to gather himself.

The crowd would thicken, and sometimes pudgy, pale cops would come by to watch and make side bets like, "Lenny, you're goin' to jail if I lose another fifty on you!"

I never gambled on junkie fights, but I'd always watch. Duncan couldn't care less; he'd scrape the block for more sales. He'd serve your customers while you were goofing off and watching the match. Duncan had a relentless money-making approach, rarely joking, never killing time, and only finding joy in hitting his sales quota, which changed daily, just like the staff on our corners.

"Dat nigga done! Dat nigga done!" was the usual chant when Lenny couldn't get back up. I saw Loraine beat Lenny's ass a thousand times.

I remember one time when Lenny had a "Rocky" moment— he lunged forward with an overhand right that connected perfectly with Loraine's chin, and she swallowed the blow like a small pill and finished him off with two to the gut and a firm hook that stood him straight up before laying him out like school clothes. She then picked him up as always and gently placed him on a stoop like an infant before claiming her prize—$20 worth of crack and some high fives from us. The guys on the block I hustled with lived for these fights, or dope fiend races, or drinking contests, or anything else they could bet on, and most of these events ended the same. The losers trading money for cheap shots from the winners, as we all reported back to our posts.

The hustlers would go back to hustling, the police would go back to policing, and the junkies would go back to chasing. We all worked all day.

A year or so later, Loraine overdosed while Lenny was in prison or rehab or both. Either way, he came back to the same corner as a transformed person. Lenny had doubled in size since the days when his wife used to beat the shit out of him, and his bumpy Braille-textured skin looked surprisingly clear and smooth, like he modeled for Neutrogena or something. Another hustler offered him a free rock as a coming-home gift, and Lenny proudly declined as he shook a fist full of multicolored NA key chains at us.

"No junk in a year, shorty, I'm off dat shit for good!" he cheered. I clapped for him and gave him a few twenties as a coming-home gift. We thought he'd be back.

Lenny landed a job working for the city but loved to stop by the corner and holler at us. "Boy I sucks up allll the overtime! Check gonna be fatter than a project cockroach!" he'd say to us after late shifts.

When not working overtime, he cut hair, or at least he tried, and fed his new addiction for gold rings. He'd cover every finger. His hands looked like he was wearing brass knuckles. But more important, Lenny stayed clean and remained that way until he died.

Witnessing his transformation was one of the early factors that led me to believe I could beat the streets, too. Lenny once pulled me aside and said, "Boy, you can make money doing anything if you work hard and good at it." I don't remember the context of the conversation, but the phrase stuck with me as I transitioned from dealer to student.

Now, as a college grad, I still frequent the neighborhood as an example of someone who exited the drug game. And even though my student loan debt is high enough to push me into drug addiction, I'm happy to represent the redemptive power of education. Proof that shows that if I can do it, you can, too.

My close friend Darnell Baylor works in the same east Baltimore neighborhood, too, as a psychiatric rehabilitation program worker. His job is to counsel juvenile offenders—making sure they go to school and keep their parole dates and occasionally taking them on field trips. I've been to work with him a few times—into the homes of the fatherless clients his agency pays him to visit. At times, he's the only positive male these young men see. The agency doesn't pay Darnell to take on this fatherly role.

They also don't pay him to make sure the kids can eat when the welfare runs out or to get them haircuts or sneakers so they don't get teased and tempted to sell. They don't pay him to enroll these young men in sports and after-school programs. They don't pay him to take his clients to the National Great Blacks in Wax Museum or Walters Art Gallery on his off days, where he exposes them to different cultures and the role models needed to stay out of prison. They don't pay him to reward his clients when they excel in school by treating them to Baltimore Ravens games. Darnell's heart is bigger than both of the shoulders that he uses to lift his community.

Darnell applies the same work ethic to his 9-to-5 that a street kid like Lil Duncan had on the corner, and it's hard to believe that a person who is not a corporation, a group, or a movement can have such an impact on an entire community. One day over drinks, I asked Darnell how he does so much, and he simply responded with, "I don't even know, but I make a way because it's right."

There's a tattered house in the same community where Darnell Baylor works. It looks like it's impatiently waiting to be torn down and could easily pass for abandoned. An anonymous woman in a crinkled shower cap tilts half of her head out of the second-story window all day—overlooking Darnell and me, drug transactions, police brutality, playing kids, pregnant teens, plump rats, hoop tournaments, dancing fiends, evangelizing Christians, and everything else that goes on in our hood or any hood.

I don't know if she has a disability or some sort of ailment, but I know she works all day. I saw her shower cap at 8 a.m., and I also saw the moon reflection bouncing off the same cap around midnight as well. Any time between those hours, you'll see kids walk up to her window and use hand signals to show the amount of candy they want. She then reels down an old cloudy pencil pack attached to about 8 feet of tied-together shoestrings. The kids dump their loose change into the pack and anxiously wait as she reels it up and then sends the stuffed pouch of goodies back down to them. She creates the same feeling for adults with loose cigarettes. And the list goes on and on.

The fact is that I can travel through east Baltimore or any urban inner city (black) neighborhood for under ten minutes and introduce you to the hardest-working Americans in our country. I know a guy who guts houses for $50 a day, a rack of uncertified tax preparers, too many single moms with triple jobs, some freelance freelancers, infinite party promoters, squeegee kids, basement caterers, back-alley auto mechanics, dudes of all ages selling bottled water, and a collection of Mr. Fix Its, all living in a two-block radius. We are all American dream chasers, all trying to start our own business, all working our asses off.

Legal or illegal, the inner cities of America are our nation's hotbed of side hustles. Even people like me with college degrees need multiple streams of revenue to survive, and I gained that work ethic from living in the inner city. Seeing my grandma work ten-hour shifts showed me I could do the same.

There are a million grinding grandmas like mine, and Darnell Baylor isn't the only person who gets paid for forty hours a week but works eighty. Every person I know is humping it, and he or she gained that work ethic from growing up in the inner city. If Lil Duncan had been exposed to a different way of life, he'd probably be running a Fortune 500 company today. Lenny and Loraine didn't beg for drugs, they performed for them. And Lenny continued to work hard years after his crack addiction faded. The Candy and Cigarette Lady should be celebrated for her shoestring enterprise. And I'd bet that even if the cops rushed in and busted her startup, her work ethic and creativity would lead her to create a new one.

There are so many hardworking people like us who are forced to create our own industries as a direct result of being isolated by society. To me, that poses a bigger question. Why is employment inequality for African Americans always identified as laziness?

Hire us.

That Yak Will Kill You: Rollin' with My Uncle and His Homeboy Rod

The drug laws in America are more ridiculous than a Tea Party diversity rally. The fact that marijuana, a natural plant that comes from the earth, remains illegal in most states while poisonous alcohol is available for purchase on almost every city corner is beyond me. My uncle taught me the difference between the two way back in the '90s.

When summer hit, I used to cover my rolled-up tube socks with the scuffed Air Jordans that guided my ashy-bony preteen body up and down Monument Street. My friends and I would walk, run, skip, and wheelie past Lakewood and Bradford and keep on going until we reached Patterson Park. There, my uncle and his homeboys posted up with their Sergio sweats, Fila, bike shorts, and gold chains. They laughed, they pointed, they screamed, they slapboxed, they made plans, they threw dice, they traded money, and they got their cars washed. He and his homeboys were getting their cars washed almost every time I saw them, even when it rained. My uncle used to hold his Henny bottle high over his head like a championship trophy. The two were inseparable. That bottle was a part of his uniform, always by his side and even dark-brown complicated—just like him.

Most of those dudes on the corner smoked weed and guzzled alcohol—except my uncle and his homeboy Rod. My uncle wouldn't touch weed because he had a job that piss-tested regularly and his homeboy Rod didn't drink alcohol because it was poison. I'd go to the corner store to grab red plastic cups, Chick-O-Sticks, and blunts for them—coming back to slow rants led by Rod, like, "Man, I'm telllllllin you, that liquor will kill you. I can smoke a ounce and be good, but if you finish that fifth you'll die cuz yak is poison, my brova."

My uncle would wave him off, pour some in the cup, take a swig from the bottle, pass the bottle, down the cup, reach for the bottle again, pour a drip out on the curb for the dead homies, and then spill some into his cold cup all over again.

Rod would shake his head in despair, while he'd split a White Owl with his ring finger, dumping the blunt guts by the curb and then re-stuffing the cracked cigarillo with fluffy green buds that were covered in orange hairs.

Rod didn't have to worry about my uncle drinking the whole fifth and dying of alcohol poisoning because my uncle never finished a whole bottle. He was a monster after a few cups, and his tolerance never picked up.

I started clubbing with them by the time I turned fifteen. They both had about ten years on me and were cool enough to get me into adult nightspots like Hammerjacks and Club Fahrenheit. But my uncle's drinking made partying with them old for me by the time I was two weekends in.

Weekend one starred my uncle, two shots of Hennessy, and the squeezing of some random girl's ass. The bouncers didn't find his advances funny and threw him out the front door ass first. Rod smooth-talked the club manager and the bouncers so that my uncle wouldn't be thrown in jail. My uncle lay dormant in the back seat of his own car. I rolled a blunt while Rod drove me home, and we both ashed in the half cup that my uncle left in the car.

On weekend two, my uncle and Hennessy picked a fight with some dudes from Park Heights. We were five deep in a packed club, and I swear it felt like everybody else in the building was from Park Heights because I've never been hit with so many uppercuts and Timberland boots at once in my life. Two of the dudes who rolled with us ran—and me, my uncle, and his homeboy Rod fought three on fifty. The cops rushed and beat on us some more, but I made it home. I woke up at Rod's that next day. We all had lumpy faces and rings around our eyes like raccoons. My uncle was filling the toilet with vomit as Rod dug in a weed sack, placed a handful of bud on the table and proceeded to roll—I joined in.

Stories of my uncle's brawls picked up as the years went by. His actions got so bad that Rod stopped hanging with him. Worse than his tirades and melees was his physical appearance. Is this what alcohol does? His once-tight face puffed and sagged now. He was still thin, but his belly poked out, and his eyes were always piss yellow. More surprisingly, his homeboy Rod looked the same as he always had.

Observing my uncle and his homeboy over the years has led me to conclude that even though alcohol's legal, it makes you mean, belligerent, loud, obnoxious, and crazy—all while making you look ten years older and destroying your liver. Weed, which remains illegal in many places, makes you over-analytical, think deeply about shallow stuff, and maybe a little sleepy.

And even the simplest Google search brings tons of research proving alcohol is far more dangerous. The scholarly journal *Addictive Behaviors* reported, "Alcohol is clearly the drug with the most evidence to support a direct intoxication-violence relationship," whereas, "Cannabis reduces the likelihood of violence during intoxication." And the US Department of Health and Human Services estimates that 25 to 30 percent of violent crimes and 3 to 4 percent of property crimes in the United States are linked to the use of alcohol. According to a report from the US Department of Justice, that translates to nearly a half million alcohol-related violent crimes per year. By contrast, the government does not even track violent acts specifically related to marijuana use, as the use of marijuana has not been associated with violence.

It's obvious that America leaves marijuana illegal as a ploy to feed its ever-so-lucrative prison industrial complex—I guess the real question I should be asking myself is why do I drink?

Gunplay Is All I Know

The other night, I got one of those 3 a.m. phone calls I hate. My homie Tip was on the other end, like, "Wake the fuck up! Yo, you ain't gonna believe this shit!"

"Who got hit now?" I headed to the fridge, in search of a little wine or vodka or something to numb the blow I knew was coming. I know how this works.

"Free, yo! They killed Free!"

"Free! Free?" I was just with Free the other week. We leaned on the fence at Bocek Park, watching wiry teens battle it out in a game of 50 on the court, laughing at how our hoop dreams faded.

"What happened, yo?" I replied, pouring the last of the Svedka into my cup.

Tip said some kids were arguing, one slid off, came back, and sprayed the whole corner. When everyone came out of hiding, Free was lying on the ground face-first in a pool of blood with a big hole in his head. The argument had nothing to do with him; he was just in the wrong place at the wrong time.

I chugged my drink. It wasn't enough to give me a buzz and definitely not enough to cover the hole that Free's death had left.

Death hurts. East Baltimore guys like us hide behind our male bravado and pretend to be desensitized by murder, but it's not really true. The thought of Free being gone left a pain in my chest that spread as I moved from room to room. Three gulps into another bottle of Svedka, and I still felt the same.

Free wasn't supposed to be murdered. He was a forty-something-year-old dude who worked for the city. Free had two daughters he loved dearly. He wasn't a gangsta, just a regular guy who loved ladies and greasy chicken cheese steaks with extra provolone from Mama Mia's. I don't even remember Free breaking the law. He was that older dude who hung around my friends and me when we sold smack on Durham Street back in the day. He'd crack jokes with us and hit on every woman who walked by, like, "No disrespect, but you lookin' good today, Boo Boo!"

And now he's gone.

A day or so after his death, I went and chilled on the same steps where he was hit. The blood had dried, and people had left teddy bears. Balloons that read I LOVE YOU and RIP FREE were taped to a street lamp. Slumped faces decorated the murder scene with red cups and lit Newports. Some T-shirts with Free's face began to pop up. Every conversation on the corner that day began with "Remember when Free . . ."

A few weeks ago, I had a photo shoot with *The Baltimore Sun*. A local reporter named Julie Scharper was doing a story on my journey from reckless delinquent to published writer. I decided to have the photo for the article taken in front of Bocek Park, not too far from where Free was murdered.

The camera guy drove by slowly and squinted as I waved, giving him the signal that I was the guy waiting for him. He paralleled his hybrid, exited, and dragged his equipment my way.

"My apologies, sir. Who are you again, and why am I taking your picture for the *Sun*?"

I told him about my rough upbringing and the events that led up to me leaving a life of crime. His eyes welled but didn't spill. He was proud, and said stories like mine gave him hope.

Some days before my shoot, he had to document a candlelight vigil for a fourteen-year-old kid named Najee Thomas, who took a shot in the head in the Cherry Hill area of south Baltimore. While there, he saw a small boy ask his mom, "Why did they kill Najee? He was a good guy!" His mom nodded and said, "That's just how it is."

The *Sun* photographer looked me in the eyes. "Does it really have to be like that?" he asked.

I couldn't answer his question. I never consider myself to be a shooter, but gunplay is all I know.

At eleven, my cousin Don Don was murdered over a girl he didn't really date, named Tracy. It was a Sunday, and we had all been watching *Martin* before spilling onto the corner and imitating Otis, Sheneneh, and the rest of the characters from the show. Tracy's insanely jealous ex and an accomplice rained on our joy with blue flames. We scattered like roaches under a flicked light. When the smoke cleared, a teenage girl was hit in the back, and Don Don was left staring lifeless beyond the clouds. His eyes were hollow, his shirt drenched with blood, which eventually smeared on us as we formed a preteen circle around his body, begging him to wake up. Cops pulled us away as ambulance workers covered him with a white sheet, his neon Nikes poking out.

Don Don wasn't the first or the last. When I was fourteen, I wrote a twenty-page paper for my history class titled, "My Baltimore: The 15 times I Was Almost Murdered." The paper gave a detailed account of the murders I saw and the shots I ducked. My history teacher, Mr. Brown, said, "I never thought I could give an A to a paper with so many grammatical errors, but the eastside is real!"

That same year, my friends and I attended lusty preteen house parties every week. Baltimore club music ripped out of blown speakers while we grinded up against the prettiest-roundest-fastest-girls from our neighborhood. New sneakers got stepped on all night, but we didn't care. We just wanted to be noticed by the girls we dreamed about all day. But egos led to more than one party being shot up. A group of dudes who called themselves "The Regulators" were the first to pop pistols at our house party, followed by weekly shootouts between multiple crews. We didn't stop going. We brought our guns out, too.

Pistols became part of our uniforms. We toted them religiously to our basketball games, the shopping mall, and everywhere else we went.

It's easier to get a gun than a job in east Baltimore. I went to Fat Hands's and Naked's crib with $300 and came out with a two-toned .45 that had a cracked safety. For a few more hundreds, I could've gotten a Glock or a dirty Desert Eagle.

And dudes with thousands to blow could cop vest, 50-shot Macs with cooling kits, HKs or AR-15s—I didn't need all of that, my four-fifth held me down through the bulk of my high school years. I aimed it at my own intense eyes in the mirror and imagined pulling the trigger as a hero or protector.

Oversize clothes helped me conceal as I trudged through three of the most dangerous neighborhoods in the city to get to my school. I almost missed prom because I misplaced my gun and wasn't going without a strap. My friend and our dates were outside yelling, slamming the horn, like, "Hurry the fuck up! That picture line gonna be long as shit!"

They forgave me when I explained what happened. Imagine slow dancing with your high school crush, while trying not to drop your pistol, gat, hammer, ratchet, son, tool, torch, banger, flamer, iron, steel, biscuit, Roscoe, heat, burner, or whatever we called it at the time.

I thank God I never had to use it. We weren't killers and didn't even think about dealing at the time. We were just scared kids who didn't want to lie dead in the streets like our brothers, fathers, friends, and the rest of the black dudes who get murdered all over the country.

A frican American males are being hunted from multiple directions. We kill each other, we are killed by sociopaths like George Zimmerman, Dylann Roof, and Michael Dunn, and then there's the cops.

Officer Friendly was the only hero cop I ever met. He spoke at my school back when I was seven. He'd come through with a big grin, give a speech about saying no to drugs, and even shared his doughnuts and juice afterward. He made being a cop seem honorable, like a job based on helping people. A guy you could call or lean on for anything at any time.

Within a few years, Officer Friendly turned into Officer Asshole and multiplied by thousands. He never came back to our schools.

He and his gang of blue uniformed dickheads would invade our neighborhood kicking in doors, robbing drug dealers, clothes-lining us off our dirt bikes, cursing out church grandmas, not sharing their doughnuts, spitting at our food, and cracking the shit out of anyone who disagreed, leaving me to believe that cops hated me, even when I was an innocent kid. I knew cops hated me when I was a notorious dope dealer, and now they hate me as a law-abiding, taxpaying citizen who pulls kids off the corner. I can't remember a time when I wasn't being harassed or profiled.

Last fall, I was walking around the neighborhood with Nathan Corbett, an actor who played Donut in HBO's *The Wire*. We were walking a scooter down my alley. A city truck burst into the opposite side, almost knocking us over. The driver glanced at us, saw we were okay, and kept moving. Nate continued walking as I waved my middle finger toward their rearview. Seconds later, we hit my garage, and I began to slide my key into the lock.

"GET THE FUCK ON THE GROUND! SHOW YOUR HANDS!"

I dropped my keys as Nate yelled, "What the fuck!" Two white cops with beet-red skin aimed pistols at us.

"Why are you breaking into that house? Where is your ID?" said the shorter, redder one.

Nate told the cops his dad was a cop, and they yelled for IDs again. I told them I owned the house and they inched forward, index fingers massaging their triggers. My neighbors watched without saying a word, which was just as disturbing to me as these officers.

"He's a fucking actor, and I'm a teacher. Go chase real crooks and leave us the fuck alone!" I yelled. I dropped my wallet on the ground and kicked it toward him. He looked at my Hopkins student

ID and said, "Oh Hopkins, must be nice," while giving his partner that "they check out" nod.

The taller cop tucked his gun as he said, "Stay out of trouble!" They left my ID on the ground and didn't apologize.

And this type of shit happens every day, especially in Baltimore. Bullets have no name, professions are irrelevant, age doesn't matter, and anyone can be shot. One false move, and any one of these officers could've decorated my garage door with my and Nate's blood.

Murder culture seems to be as permanent in African American culture as hip-hop, cookouts, and the black church. I see young Chicago rappers like RondoNumbaNine, L'A Capone (who died last year), and Chief Keef waving pistols on most of their rap videos and then see more established acts like Beyoncé and Jay Z doing the same to promote their tour. And then I see murder on the news, normally before walking out of my front door and seeing the same. Real or fake, everybody is slinging pistols—and being young and black makes owning one mandatory.

I'm not a gangster and could not care less about weapon shows or trips to a shooting range, but I have two guns. I don't want them, but I need them to protect my family. I need them for the multiple Second Amendment abusers who foolishly think pulling a trigger isn't cowardly. I need them because the murderers of African Americans are a diverse group. And most important, I need them because the media and mainstream America only get emotional over mass suburban shootings that involve non-blacks, while we are in slums getting popped every day.

I'm naive to be surprised by Free's murder. Or my cousin Damon who was thirty-six, my friend Nard who was twenty-four, or Dev at twenty, or DI at seventeen, or Bip at eighteen, or Man Man at sixteen, or Bryant at twelve, or Don Don at twenty-two, or LA at thirty-five, or the countless other people I could name.

I'm still in east Baltimore, and even though I signed a book deal, I'm nowhere near rich, and my essays can't block bullets. I still frequent some of the worst neighborhoods in my city because that's my home, where I live, and where all my family and friends reside.

I could easily be Free. I could easily be sitting out on Caroline Street on a nice summer day smashing some fried lake trout and collards without a fork when a Chevy Corsica bends the corner and lights the block up like July 4.

Any day, I could be in the wrong place at the wrong time catching slugs that are meant for another person who looks just like me, from another person who looks just like me. Some woman would scream, "That's my baby!" I'd get a small mention in the obituary section or maybe a larger write-up because of my Internet fame. My good friends would light blunts and pour out a little liquor, and just like the dudes before me, my face would glow on T-shirts and all over Instagram. There would be teddy bears, balloons, and empty liquor bottles decorating the corner where I had my last meal.

The hood would mourn, and then it would happen again.

And again and again.

Black Women

On the first hot day of 2015, a woman and her child walked past the tiny corner of Curley and Madison in east Baltimore. Bulk chants of "Ohhhh! Got Damn! Smile baby! Shorty you phat as shit! Bring dat ass over here!" ripped from the corner where about thirty of us stood: thirty different guys, with thirty different occupations, all brought up in the same abrasive culture where many men feel entitled to women.

"Chill man, leave her alone!" I yell. My friend T echoes, "Yeah man, she don't want ya'll bums anyway!"

The woman stops and muffles her child's ears, "Ya'll some fuckin' clowns!" and continues down the block.

Most of the dudes bust out in laughter; some of us shake our heads in despair. One dude mixed up in our group, a light-skinned kid with one big gold tooth, speaks out, saying, "Yo that's why I only fuck wit white women now—black ones be too angry!"

Don't they have a right to be?

Black women have been feeling the heel of America's boot since the first slave ships arrived to North America. Stepping foot off of the boat guaranteed a number of horrible things, including being sold, raped, humiliated, bred like show dogs, separated from their children, beaten, overworked, or all of the above on constant repeat.

Generations and generations of slaves who provided the free labor responsible for America's superpower status all made their way into the country via black vagina. And how do we repay these women? How we do repay black women for birthing our nation? We don't—we just sit back and allow them to be treated like third-class citizens?

Third class because our society already treats blacks and women like second-class citizens. Black women have to remain resilient while enduring a combined discrimination.

It's never been my style, but dudes have been hollering, cat-calling, or cracking on women years before I was even born. Maybe they think it's a filter for weaning out women with high standards, fig-uring that one out of fifty women who respond will automatically be an easy lay. That's not for me to judge, but I grew up in east Baltimore dope-boy culture where the coolest guys attracted women by dressing nice, being popular, and having conversations. Screaming at women and acting thirsty always looked stupid to me and always will. Seeing the look on that young woman's face while she was walking with her child made me realize how scary it can be for a woman to walk down the street.

For insight, I interviewed activist Juliana Pache, cofounder of Pussy Power, a Philly-based feminist group with the purpose of creating spaces where women can feel safe and free to express themselves.

Pache says, "I almost always cross the street if I see a big group of men." Being around crowds of men is often scary to me in bars and parties. Sometimes men are really aggressive. The difference between the street and the club, in my experience, is that on the street, men more often harass verbally; in the club, men harass physically. Currently Pussy Power is brainstorming ideas on how to tackle violence against women in club/party environments in the Philadelphia area.

T fills a red plastic cup with Ciroc and says, "Yo, she had her son with her!" I chime in, "What if somebody said, 'Lemme squeeze your sexy fat ass' to your grandma? Would that be cool?"

The light-skinned kid shrugs. Travis, the tallest kid out there answers, "Yo, little man gotta learn the game. One day he'll yell at somebody's sister on the street!"

And that's the problem. Remaining silent and following suit is how our misogynistic culture sustains for generations. Little guys see big guys street harass and then grow up to street harass, and this toxic tradition is so strong that the kid in front of me shrugs at the idea of me telling his grandma that she has a sexy fat ass. How?

I don't know his grandma, but I'm sure she's like my late granny or any other black grandma who has been and forever will be the MVPs of the black community. Despite the mountainous disparities they face, black women have been the only consistent people in my neighborhood. It's like they never fail. They keep a job, a roof, and a surplus of food while being the glue that holds our unstable lives together. I know this, and these guys know it, too, which is why their actions disgust me.

"Man, y'all sound like Captain Save-a-hoes!" says Travis, pulling a Black-N-Mild from his ear and sparking it. "Lemme get y'all some capes!" Everyone laughs.

T yells over the crowd, "Yelling at women on the street don't work, so why do it! Yo Travis on some real shit! I never even saw you with a girl—you ain't have pussy since pussy had you!" The laughing shifts from us to Travis.

"Men should call each other out when they see their friends violating women," Pache says. "They should sit them down and explain to them how wrong they are. Just like white people need to call each other out on racism. If you are in a privileged group, and you want to help oppressed people, one of the best things you can do is teach other people in your privileged group. As a person of privilege, you do not have to actually face the oppression, so you have time to teach. Oppressed people do not have the energy to teach everyone about the oppression they have to live through every day."

I push to the front, instantly commanding the attention of the group and reminding most of them of who they live with, whose cell phone account they're on, who feeds them or fed them when they were flat broke, who brought them into the world, who let them stay on the basement couch past the age of thirty, who raised them, who they call when they get in trouble, who co-signs, who got that bail money, who was there when everyone else bailed, and how, when trouble strikes, "Mommy!" is the first thing they always yell out.

Some fake like it's not true, but most nod, acknowledging that their go-to people are always their black grandmothers, black wives, black girlfriends, black sisters, and black daughters.

I asked Pache how we move forward. "Privileged groups should stop expecting oppressed groups to teach them. We're busy being oppressed. The whole concept that privileged people won't learn unless we teach them is just pure laziness. If you care about the people around you, you'll do the work to educate yourself."

Educating and making myself aware of the issues that many of the women in my community face is only half the battle. In the song "Keep Ya Head Up," 2Pac had said something like, we all came from a woman and got our most precious gifts from women. So why do we hate and abuse our women? It's time, said 2Pac, to turn it around and start loving our women again. Pac had it right; we men are responsible for not only stopping guys from harassing women but also telling others to do the same, for this is the only way to shift the culture.

Rappers' Blood Diamonds

Weeks after William Leonard Roberts, better known by the stage name Rick Ross, won his case in a battle over the name with the real Rick Ross, my eleven-year-old nephew Karl and his bugged eyes ran up on me with some Ross rap music. He was all excited, like, "Uncle D, Rick Ross is the biggest drug dealer ever, he's so G, he only raps for a hobby because he already made millions moving crack!"

My nephew never sold a drug in his life because of me. *Sell a drug and I'll whip your ass* is what I beat into his reality; however, he is still from east Baltimore, and I can't stop that. Being from east Baltimore means that you are biologically programmed to be infatuated with drug culture—who's getting money, who's snitching, who has the best dope, who's driving what, who murdered who, and so forth.

"So Karl," I say.

"K. Dot, uncle D. Call me K. Dot!"

"So K. Dot, you know Rick Ross isn't the real Rick Ross, right?"

He goes on to tell me how Rick Ross is a master of stretching coke. How he takes one kilogram of cocaine and morphs it into three or four or five, maximizing his profits far beyond anything we could ever comprehend.

"So Ross to coke is kinda like Jesus with the making water into wine thing?"

"Exactly. You're my favorite uncle because you get it!" he yells, overpowering my car's sound system, drowning out the Jay Electronica I'd been listening to all week. I let K. Dot cut Ross on. His beats knock, and he and his MMG (Maybach Music Group) crew have amazing energy. They're the best in rap right now. K. Dot is bopping his head as we cruise, feeling the vibe and reciting every lyric as his neck makes yes-like motions. I wonder if he knows that he's affirming every idea that comes out of the speakers.

"Yeah, K. Dot, I get it," I say, cutting off the music. "Rick Ross is an ex-correctional officer who bounced around from label to label until he found a home at Def Jam. He may not be a real gangster. Your real family, some of our cousins and uncles are GD (Gangsta Disciples) connected—the gang that made Ross cancel paid tours. That's a penalty for being a poser. You can't yell GD unless you are GD!"

"Really? No guns? Ross fought back, right?" asked K. Dot.

"Nope. He has millions of legal dollars, he'd be a fool to fight back. Ross received around-the-clock support from his paid bodyguards and the Miami Police Department. No beef, no guns, and no war. Rick Ross is only connected with two gangs: MMG and the police department."

I Google the image of Rick Ross looking all thick and snug and happy in his old CO uniform and then passed my phone to K. Dot. His eyes glaze over, his face slumps past his chest. I broke his spirit. I had to; it was a must.

"So the real Rick Ross, not the rap star, made millions moving tons of cocaine with connections that led all the way up to the White House—and then spent more than two decades in federal prison," I add.

"Damn!" yells K. Dot, no longer slouching. He's embracing a new hero, seamlessly dismissing the old one.

And now I have to teach K. Dot that the other Ross is flawed as well.

The rapper Rick Ross is caught up in the same drug nostalgia that hypnotizes a countless number of teens. The problem is that the rapper is only selling a half-truth—probably because, like many rappers, he's a witness and not a player.

The story of the witness is valuable—but people like me who have played this deadly game at multiple levels need to be responsible for identifying the difference. Rappers like Ross and many others only focus on the heaven that comes with selling—the cars, the cash, the girls, and the shootout victories. All of their drug songs end in heaven.

I'm well aware of that heaven. I sold crack and heroin for years after high school. Cash-filled Nike boxes were under my bed, I had no shortage of friends, and I drove every car imaginable.

Maintaining that lifestyle was the hell that many rappers neglect to reference. Working one-hundred-plus hours a week, burying best friends, and seeing their moms cry and feeling their tears spill on you are hell. Being beat on by beat cops is hell. Looking at that shoebox full of cash under your bed and noticing the shoebox full of obituaries next to it is hell.

Your aunts and friends' mothers hitting you up for free crack so they won't have to turn tricks or sell their kids' toys is hell. Seeing them smoke the drugs you give them is hell. Watching people who look identical to you die is hell; that two-year-old girl catching that stray bullet over drug territory is hell.

K. Dot being infatuated with the heaven and not fully understanding the other side is hell.

Ichallenge drug rappers to add more depth to their raps by acknowledging those hells. They need to give the negative side equal representation by telling listeners that most dealers aren't living the high life. By telling them that Jay Z or Ross never purchased Lamborghinis from violent crack money, that it was rap money that made those cars a reality. And those music biz fortunes are too often generated by songs that romanticize the drug hustle.

Rappers need to tell listeners the truth—that most dealers are broke and can't afford child support and barely have enough to pay their Sprint bill after buying new product to sell. The truth is that crack is almost as obsolete as typewriters and that no one is making millions off of it except the artists who get checks from singing about it.

In the end, why can't we celebrate that? Why can't we celebrate Ross as a talented young black man who has made millions from his art? As a person who took his destiny into his own hands, created an empire, and employed street people who probably couldn't get jobs under different circumstances?

I once heard Ross say, "How many people you bless is how you measure success!" I thought that was great, but I'm in the streets daily, and the glamorous depiction of drug dealing put forth by many rappers isn't blessing anyone.

It's killing black kids.

The School of Failure

My 13-year-old nephew Butta was getting into trouble weekly. Arguing with teachers, ignoring administrators, and walking out of class. It got to the point where my sister had a time-block in her schedule every month dedicated to parent–teacher conferences—but they didn't work.

Butta is as harmless as he is plump—that jolly kid who loves to split up his chips between his friends and would gladly give you the last bite of his sandwich. He's never been in trouble outside of school, which says a lot, since his dad, the rest of his uncles, and I had all been arrested or kicked out of a school at least once by the time we reached his age.

"What's going on with your classes?" I asked him.

"My teachers hate me, and they throw me in wit Mr. Ronald, that sub who be on his phone all day, talkin' about he don't need this job, cuz he got his own company! He ain't got no company!"

Butta's in middle school, so he should have more than one teacher. But they throw all the troubled kids in one class with a long-term substitute teacher all day, where they are allowed to shoot dice, play cards, IG, Tweet, Facebook, dance, stand on desks, and basically do whatever they please. I've been guilty of pushing subs around—everybody taunts the sub when the normal teacher is absent—but these kids have been doing this for months.

Everyone knows how tough the middle schools in Baltimore are. I recently had a conversation with Stacey Cook, a former teacher from James McHenry Elementary/Middle School in south Baltimore, and she told me that they had multiple shootings last year, right in front of their building during school hours. "One day the gym teacher was almost caught in the crossfire. He hit the buzzer, fearing for his life, begging to be let in. But the principal waited until the shooting stopped. He said we knew where we were, and that's how it is. The gym teacher, me, and a bunch of other educators left at the end of the year."

I'm grateful that no one has shot up my nephew's school, but his learning experience was still criminal. Being trapped in a room for six-plus hours a day, surrounded by chaos and a sub fingering his phone sounds illegal.

I thought that Butta and his teachers probably had a communication problem that I could mediate. A lot of inner-city teachers are used to dealing with just one parent, if any—I wanted to be the objective voice considering all points of view with the hope of helping him develop a working relationship with his teacher and getting back on track, so I decided to visit.

My sister and I pulled up in front of his school on a Monday. It looked clean from the outside and was located on a nice tree-lined block. We were buzzed into a narrow hallway. Three huge school officers in small uniforms clogged the path. They looked like prison guards. The built-in metal detector was cracked and unplugged, so in prison fashion one of the guards scanned us with a wand while another checked our credentials. We passed their test and were directed to the main office, a level up at the end of the same hallway.

The stairwell smelled like used rubbers and rat piss. Blunt guts, unidentifiable fluids, and candy wrappers laced the floor. I stepped over all of that and made my way to the office. Some concerned-looking parents and guardians were present, probably trying to see what it would take to make sure their kids received a quality education—the same thing I wanted to do for Butta.

We greeted the secretary. She seemed nice, remembered my sister, and instructed us to sign in before sending us up to Butta's class. That same funky smell in the stairwell greeted us again as we advanced another level.

This school seemed like a jail, and level two—Butta's floor— was the psych ward. Students bolting up and down the hallways, desks taking flight, a trail of graded and ungraded papers scattered everywhere, fight videos being recorded on cell phones, Rich Homie Quan blasting at the highest decibel, crap games and card games going down with children named Bitch and Fuckyou everywhere—all bottled up and sealed with that same shitty smell, so bad it was loud enough to hear, a shit stench I hoped wouldn't stick to my flannel.

"So this is it," my sister says with an uneasy smirk. This is her only option. She's raising Butta alone, and even though we all chip in, private school is still too expensive. Butta's classroom was an east Baltimore block party: slam-dancing, students leaping from tabletop to tabletop, and one of the substitutes Butta talked about texting and Facebooking. A main goal for our visit was to get Butta away from the texting sub and back to his real teacher, but she was gone that day anyway—stomped down and beat up, we later learned, by eighth-grade girls mad after she confiscated their cell phones.

It's hard to receive a good education in this environment. I'd be hard pressed to believe a good teacher could be effective. The computers were ancient, the textbooks were decayed, and the classroom felt like it was 15 degrees Fahrenheit—thirty to thirty-five musky, puberty-drenched kids and it was still cold. How can you learn in the cold? How can we be in the United States, in 2014, in a major metropolitan city and not have temperature-controlled classrooms? I mean, the main office was nice and cozy, so why were the classrooms meat freezers?

Not that I was surprised. My middle school experience had been identical, from the smell and lack of technology to the overworked and/or disengaged teachers who turned into a sub-hub by mid-year. Add that learning experience to the idea of being educated in a war zone. My story in conjunction with Butta's does nothing but follow a long tradition of the African American educational experience in the United States.

Back in the late 1990s, my all-American, apple-pie-faced middle school history teacher used to put us to sleep with his month-long patriotic rants. He would gaze into the sky and tell stories about how the United States was the only place where you could come bearing nothing but your religion and a dream and experience an inexhaustible amount of success. I got the concept of dreaming, but my ancestors came here bearing only fear, chains, and uncertainty. They were not people in search of hope but captives forced to cultivate and construct the so-called free world.

While African slaves spent countless days cooking, cleaning, being raped, beaten, sweating in the fields, and occasionally lynched, the children of their rich masters were being educated. The 1800s saw schools pop up all over the United States, and by the end of the 19th century, free public education was available for all white children. Blacks have been in America since 1619 and received virtually no schooling until after President Abraham Lincoln decreed the Emancipation Proclamation in 1863. That is a 244-year head start given to whites—244 years of exposure to scientific reasoning and philosophical thought, hundreds of years to discover the power of books and reading and to shape dreams into reality.

"There's a myth floating around that education is white culture, books are white culture," said Eric Rice, an expert in urban education, when I went to visit him at the Johns Hopkins University School of Education this year. "But African Americans have a long history of wanting education. The South had laws against teaching slaves to read, and people risked beatings and death trying to learn to read during slavery. There has always been a huge demand."

The Lincoln administration made a conscious effort to right the wrongs in education along with other social injustices through the Freedmen's Bureau, established in 1865. Charged with clothing, feeding, employing, and otherwise helping the newly free people of color become US citizens, it even had dispensation to grant land. The Reconstruction Era in the United States, those couple of years when the South was to rebuild itself from 1865 through 1867, would have been a great time to help blacks assimilate to the dominant culture through education. For the first time, America was seeing the rise of black business owners, black politicians, and the black church, but our country didn't capitalize on the opportunity. None of that success led to a spark in black schools.

Instead, Lincoln's promises died with him that night at the theater in 1865. Andrew Johnson, the next president, vetoed the Freedmen's Bureau renewal in 1866. He confiscated the land African Americans were acquiring in the South and gave it back to the white Southerners who occupied it before the war. From 1866 to 1869, Johnson depleted the Freedmen's Bureau, which was eventually dismantled in full by his successor, Ulysses Grant, in 1872.

Sure, schools for freed slaves emerged. Within a year of emancipation, at least eight thousand former slaves began attending schools in Georgia; eight years later, those same black schools struggled to contain nearly twenty thousand students. Scores of children piled into these shacks, trying to compete while dealing with broken or no desks, leaky ceilings, and limited utensils.

"Many of the early schools for black students received hand-me-down supplies and textbooks from white schools. The class sizes were larger and the teachers had fewer qualifications. The resources devoted to black schools were fewer and lower-quality than those devoted to white schools," Rice told me. We made it into the classrooms but not on the same level.

Jim Crow laws allowing racial segregation guaranteed that the gap would widen as years passed. By the end of the 19th century, seventeen states and the District of Columbia required school segregation by law. Four others allowed the option.

That seemed poised to change when, in 1951, thirteen families from Topeka, Kansas, filed a lawsuit against their Board of Education. Like their ancestors, they wanted a quality education for their children—similar to what white children in the United States had been receiving for decades. The case came to be known as Brown v. the Board of Education and was a major victory in the fight for education for African American students. Brown v. the Board of Education showed an immense amount of promise, giving many blacks hope that America could change. The landmark Supreme Court decision of 1954 overturned the Plessy v. Ferguson verdict of 1896, which allowed state-sponsored segregation, with a 9–0 unanimous decision declaring that separate schools for blacks and whites were unconstitutional.

But the idea of blacks and whites being schooled together sent the nation into a frenzy. On June 11, 1963, George Wallace, the governor of Alabama, went as far as to stand in the doorway of the University of Alabama flanked by state troopers, so that black students couldn't get in to register, standing down only after President John F. Kennedy called in the National Guard.

"White flight" was the remedy for many Caucasians petrified by the thought that their child might share class with a Negro. They took their tax money, their resources, and their high-quality schools with them to the 'burbs. Blockbusting—the practice of pushing down property values in a neighborhood through rumors of an imminent influx of some "undesirable" group—and redlining—the practice of denying and charging more for banking services in an effort to racially construct a neighborhood—were the most publicized means of keeping the races separate. Banks' ability to approve and decline mortgages on the sole basis of color were adjuncts to the effort, as well.

So there you have it; a combination of poor schools, institutionalized segregation, and minimal funding not only cultivated the deep roots of educational denial, but also strengthened the foundation upon which achievement gaps are built today. The combination of all of these historical events led to what I call the Tradition of Failure. The tradition was not self-imposed. Obviously, African

Americans can take some personal responsibility for the state of our race; however, many of us do not have a clue because we come from a tradition of people who never had a clue, leading all the way back to the day our ancestors left Elmina, the former slave port in Ghana that launched us on our turgid journey to this new world.

They did not have a clue what was waiting for them on the other side of the Atlantic Ocean. Perhaps worse, we entered America as the lazy, ungrateful enemy without even knowing why, and it has been an uphill battle full of limitless racial and social restraints every step of the way. We didn't invent the idea of race or conceptualize the theory of free labor and what it could mean on a global scale. We just did what we were forced or told to do and have been paying the price ever since.

The biggest price has been something that even my slave ancestors might never have imagined: While education was being withheld from blacks, the prison doors were wide open and welcomed us with open arms. The Ohio State University civil rights attorney Michelle Alexander, author of *The New Jim Crow*, writes, "The criminal justice system was strategically employed to force African Americans back into a system of extreme repression and control, a tactic that would continue to prove successful for generations to come."

The pipeline from school to prison has been a hot topic in the United States and the subject of many lectures and debates. Tariq Toure, who wrote about this loop in *Black Seeds*, his poetry-memoir of inner-city Baltimore, says his own public school experience forced many of his friends into the streets. "Public schooling in America, particularly in the ghetto, particularly for Black/Brown people, is the bottling plant for mass incarceration. The decision to never invest in the tools needed to extract the genius of youth through education forces them to succumb to an already shattered environment. Ill-equipped administrations govern ill-equipped teachers thus ill-equipping masses of youth for a world that feigns to profit from their invisibility and most detrimental, their captivity," he contends. Toure thinks that pipeline schools run through poor urban communities strictly to prepare black students for prison. "Grade school should focus on investing in the inherent gifts children have. This is so far outside of the American schooling system because it approaches marginalized students from the perspective that they have no special qualities except prison survival skills."

I thought about the things I saw at Butta's school and asked about the role corporations play. "Prisons are privatized now, and a poor education in combination with other factors that exist in poor-black communities are making black failure big business [for those companies]," Toure contends. In his memoir, Toure put the dilemma facing black children in stark terms: "Public schools are prisons."

The ambience that characterized my schooling experience explains why many of the people I went to middle school with didn't make it to high school. And even though I finished, the bulk of my surroundings and influences make me feel like a transition into a life of crime is easier than reading on grade level, which sounds crazy, but it might be true.

I don't know what percentage of kids Butta's age sell drugs. But in April 2014, our hometown paper, *The Baltimore Sun*, reported our city's educational achievement: "According to the National Assessment of Educational Progress exam, only 7 percent of black boys in Baltimore City schools are reading at grade level in 8th grade. Even worse, in Maryland, 57 percent of black males are currently graduating from high school compared to 81 percent for white males.

Hundreds of black boys drop out of Baltimore high schools each year. They enter the adult world unable to read and comprehend the daily newspaper or to find a job that supports the cost of food and shelter."

Something is missing in a large number of the predominantly black schools in the United States. Whatever that missing "thing" is, the streets seem to fill the void. The streets provide an education in everything that many of these schools don't, such as survival skills, kinship, moneymaking opportunities, and love. A love that is absent from the cold hallways of schools such as the ones Butta, I, and millions of other African Americans attend or attended.

Butta's school has been shut down, along with a few other troubled city schools, since my visit. He now must attend another school in a different district full of the kids who already attended, in addition to the new students who are being packed in because their school was shut down, creating an even worse climate. Butta's new school is almost the same as his old one. He continues to receive a semi-education. Meanwhile, even more schools in Baltimore are closing this year, as Maryland's Republican Governor, Larry Hogan, prepares to slash $35 million from Baltimore Public Schools. And this isn't just a Baltimore issue. There are schools in Philadelphia that are packed with rodents and hold classes with as many as fifty students.

Too often I hear people cry, "Our schools are broken, our schools are broken!" But are they? Are our schools broken or is our system working perfectly for its creators? During the years I pursued a master of science degree in education at Johns Hopkins, I studied a theory called "social reproduction," the brainchild of a Connecticut sociologist named Christopher Doob. His theory holds that we've got to produce a certain number of minimum-wage workers and inmates—a general collection of bottom-feeders—for capitalism to sustain, and so we build the social structures to keep that level of misery going.

"Social reproduction is a real thing," Rice tells me—and although he doubts it's intentional, it's certainly convenient. "The system tends to produce the people who are needed for the jobs that will be available. We hear all of this talk on how we need to teach critical thinking because the jobs of the future will be in science, technology, engineering, mathematics, and computer science, but actually a huge number of jobs in the future will be in fast food, different service industries, and many fields that don't require critical thinking. I'm not saying that a small group of people are planning this; however, it strikes me as interesting that we continue to produce a huge number of people fit for these jobs and they tend to come out of these school systems."

Schools such as the one Butta and I attended are funded by property taxes from neighborhoods full of housing projects and boarded-up homes, where the poor pay to perpetuate their own misery. The age-old system, in conjunction with law enforcement, makes the pipeline from public school to prison a reality.

I agree with Rice; it's not a conspiracy. I'm sure we won't find a room full of rich white men plotting how to keep producing semi-educated wage slaves for their service industries and inmates for their penal empires. But I do think the system is rotten, and a fortunate few are benefiting from the degradation of the many.

I would challenge anyone who disagrees to walk through the schools in the neighborhoods where I grew up; if we don't need to fill up the prisons with more of Baltimore youth, then why don't we fix the schools now?

I applaud educational innovators such as the charter school pioneer Geoffrey Canada, who recognized the disparities in education in the African American community and made an honest attempt to address them from the bottom up by creating schools that shattered the norms. To date, his Harlem Children's Zone has produced multiple senior classes with over 92 percent four-year college acceptance rates. Many charter schools across the United States have adopted Canada's model along with other new models that focus on creating college-ready kids and have reported success. So if it works, why can't his models be adapted in all urban public school systems? Why can't we evolve pedagogy and reach for even higher levels of success?

I posed this question to Rice, who also sits on the board of two charter schools in Baltimore. "Geoffrey Canada's success has a lot to do with his ability to raise funds. He's found donors and supporters who traditionally don't want to give money to school systems. I don't know if that is a sustainable way to solve the bigger problems in entire urban districts. For me, if we really want to solve education, we need to decide to solve issues in poverty, all of the associated health problems, and employment challenges."

Rice is speaking a language that reverts right back to the root of all the educational issues our country faces. The idea that communities are structured to create generations of snubbed students who go on to create generations of snubbed students makes the idea of social reproduction real.

Revamping the public school system is just half the battle, says Celia Neustadt, founder of Baltimore's Inner Harbor Project, a nonprofit that works with schools and teens and specializes in social change. Neustadt says her project's success comes from stepping outside the system. "The young people I work with are confronted by the reality of supporting their families and keeping them safe," she says. To help such teens succeed and make it to college, a radically different toolset must be employed.

We're quick to say that the United States is a fair place where anyone can excel, but that's not true. We need to acknowledge the failure so entrenched in history we cannot see it clearly, let alone root it out. African Americans are not stupid underachievers. Our accomplishments in science, innovation, business, politics, athletics, and the arts are extraordinary—especially when you consider the countless constraints. As a matter of fact, we should be judged by our survival skills. I remember asking my friend Ron from west Baltimore about the recession after the market crashed in 2008, and he laughed: "Recession? What recession? Everything is the same round here!" In fact, for us, it was an equalizer in some ways—people outside our communities were starting to feel the pain we're used to.

We were born into a permanent recession where making $20 last a week is not a miracle—it is a way of life. Ovens are frequently used to heat up homes, everyone works under the table, and a new hustle is created every day.

A given: African Americans want to learn and be inspired like anyone else. Scholars can help bridge the achievement gaps, but only if they take the time to see what these students are up against. My own way of tackling the problem is through literacy. I want to get more people in low-income neighborhoods to develop a love for reading by creating literature that speaks directly to poverty-stricken people and encourages them to write.

But we all have a moral obligation to set things right. We are all responsible for challenging the system and forcing it to create a fair learning experience for all students because we are dealing with more than just a failed school system or a broken home, or even millions of broken homes; we are dealing with failure on a historic scale, spanning hundreds of years. Acknowledging that we face this kind of epic failure is the first step in bringing about real change. That's a big challenge in the United States, where accepting failure has never been our strength.

No one can do everything, but if we follow the Ethiopian proverb, "When spiders unite, they can tie down a lion," we'll have a better chance of solving these issues together and creating a nation that lives up to its founders' dreams of truly offering success.

My City Is Gone

Another day, another dinner. Tonight's session takes place at Food Market in Hamden. The guys who invited me represent the new Baltimore, which is full of new people, new shops, and new restaurants. They want to talk about ways I can help them understand black Baltimore—or what's left of it.

My recent collection of Baltimore writings and talks has made me the go-to guy on issues concerning the Negro culture of our city. Politicians, investors, and pretty much anyone with an interest in Baltimore request meetings with me weekly. In most of them, I trade my perspectives for potential opportunities at pricey restaurants I don't normally frequent.

Suit No. 1, who explained to me in his initial e-mail that he was a lawyer with experience working with artists, says, "This city is a gem. People here don't even know what they have!" He's new to Baltimore, so I don't expect him to know what "the people" love and value. I let him speak as Suit No. 2 nods in affirmation.

Suit No. 2 signals for another round. The restaurant is as packed as it is beautiful. A collection of affluent white grins is available along with some sprinkles of random minorities. Suit No. 1 and No. 2 look alike. Their faces aren't similar, but their dark-rimmed frames, dress code, and personalities are

identical—two know-it-all, middle-aged white dudes who probably jog daily so they can fit into their tight sport coats. I'm a
sore thumb in Food Market that night—the only patron in a
hoodie and sneakers.

The server hands us fancy drinks, and I down mine before he
can refill his tray with our empty glasses. The Suits order their steaks
extra bloody while I opt for the chicken.

"One more please," I say.

Suit No. 2 says he's a developer, says he wants to help the city,
says he isn't from Baltimore either, but he loves Baltimore. He loves
Baltimore so much—so much that he's willing to fix it! He says that
he could grow to love Baltimore as much as I do!

Thirteen-dollar cocktails tend to disappear quicker than cotton
candy in a hot mouth on a night like this. "You know what," I say,
pulling up my chair, drawing the duel in closer, "I don't really know if
I still love Baltimore."

Their eyes grow. You would've thought I just pulled my
dick out.

Suit No. 1 sounds offended. "Your writing is how I found out
about you. You are a gifted Baltimore writer. How could you not love
this place, man? How?"

"Gentri-fuckin-cation," I say. "Gentri-fuckin-cation is why I
don't know."

My city is gone, my history depleted, ruined, and undocu-
mented. I don't know this new Baltimore, it's alien to me. Baltimore is
Brooklyn and DC now. No, Baltimore is Chicago or New Orleans or
any place where yuppie interests make black neighborhoods shrink
like washed sweaters. A place where black history is bulldozed and
replaced with Starbucks, Chipotles, and dog parks.

I used to hang in Lafayette Housing Projects with my big cousin Damon. He taught me how to shoot a jump shot, impress a girl without talking, and land a left hook. That place is gone. Visiting his old unit after his murder would've been therapeutically nostalgic for me, but that place is gone and will never be back again.

And when the weather broke back in high school, my classmates and I would cut class over Somerset courts. Pooh Bear, the best baller from the neighborhood, would be knocking down jump shots from half-court on a broken rim, and I swear, I swear, I swear he rarely missed. He had everybody in the hood trying to shoot like him. We'd drop our backpacks by the gate and argue during the pickup games we played until well after sunset. Some of those arguments turned into silly fights that we quickly resolved over marijuana sticks. I'd love to walk through Somerset right now and run a 3 on 3 for old-time's sake, but that place is gone. It's a blank field; the residents are scattered like memories we once shared.

The drink has made Suit No. 1 sweat a little, but he's a trooper, he wants to do another one.

"Deeeee," he says, "new development brings new opportunity!"

"For who?" I say, a little too loud.

Really for who, who I wonder? Last summer I drove down Wolfe Street and pulled over by Eager. We called this Deakyland back in the day. Most of the earned scratches and bruises I have came from here. We used to break day at that bar High Hats that used to sit on the corner, 2Pac ripped out of speakers while our plastic cups overflowed with Hennessy—the manager Big Harold had to drag us out at 4 a.m. In between the hangovers and brawls were lessons on life, leadership, and brotherhood. We did stupid things, but that was our community, the place where our social networks were birthed and then quickly dismantled. That whole block is gone. I realized that I may never see any of those people from that place again as ten shirtless white guys played two-hand-touch football in a fresh park that they would never build for us—a huge Johns Hopkins logo was the backdrop stretched across a new parking garage.

Suit No. 2 tells me that he understands exactly where I'm coming from and can see why I feel the way I do. I ask him if he could go back to the place that holds most of the magical moments from his childhood. He says, "Yeah, my old bedroom is still the same at my folks' place."

"Then you probably don't know how I feel," I reply. "I'm lost in this city. This isn't the place I grew up in. Corporate dollars are cleansing this city of everything I loved. I will always love Baltimore, the Baltimore I grew up in. I don't know what this new place is or even if it has opportunity for me. I honestly don't even know if I should be eating here with you or down SOS on the eastside with my remaining friends. Look around. Do I really look like I belong in here?"

I understand that those now-demolished neighborhoods came with murder, pain, heartbreak, high teen pregnancy rates, illiteracy, gang violence, and a host of other reasons that led to their implosions. I also understand that all of these issues stem from lack of opportunity. However, I don't understand why every black resident must be displaced as soon as opportunity rides the gentrification train into town. To date, approximately twenty-two thousand black families have been forcibly relocated due to slum clearance, urban renewal, and highway displacement. Entire black neighborhoods have been bulldozed into thin air.

After five minutes of awkward silence, we exchange handshakes, business cards, and "Nice meeting yous" before exiting.

I drove through the city after our meeting thinking about how much I hate meetings, thinking about the new Baltimore, and wondering if my voice is even needed here anymore. I do love Baltimore, but it's becoming a place for the rich, and I don't speak their language. I passed more and more new construction before pulling up on President Street.

A wiry kid ran up to my window waving a squeegee stick just like my friends and I used to do back in the day. I rejected the wash, gave him $5 and said, "Ay Shorty, keep pushing, this will all make sense some day." He thanked me and nodded in agreement.

I wasn't sure if I was talking to him or myself.

Too Poor for Pop Culture

Miss Sheryl, Dontay, Bucket-Head, and I compiled our loose change for a fifth of vodka. I'm the only driver, so I went to get it. On the way back, I laughed at the local radio stations going on and on and on, still buzzing about Obama taking a selfie at Nelson Mandela's funeral.

Who cares?

No really, who? Especially since the funeral was weeks ago.

I arrived, fifth of Black Watch clenched close to me like a newborn with three red cold-cups covering the top. We play spades over at Miss Sheryl's place in the Douglass Housing Projects every few weeks. Her court is semi-boarded up, third world, and looks like n old ad for *The Wire*. Even though many in America would consider her complex disgustingly unfit, it's still overpopulated with tilting dope fiends, barefoot children, pregnant smokers, grandmas with diabetes, tattoo-faced tenants, and a diverse collection of Zimmermans made up of street dudes and housing police, looking itchy to shoot anyone young and black and in Nike.

Two taps on the door, it opened, and the gang was all there—four disenfranchised African Americans posted up in a 9-by-11 prison-size tenement, one of those spots where you enter the front door, take a half-step and land in the yard. I call us disenfranchised, because Obama's selfie with some random lady or the whole selfie movement in general is more important than we are and the conditions where we dwell.

Surprisingly, as tight as Miss Sheryl's unit may be, it's still more than enough space for us to receive affordable joy from a box of fifty-cent cards and a rail bottle.

"A yo, Michelle was gonna beat on Barack for taking dat selfie with dat chick at the Mandela wake! Whateva da fuck a selfie is! What's a selfie, some type of bailout?" yelled Dontay from the kitchen, dumping Utz chips into a cracked, flowery bowl. I was placing cubes into all of our cups and equally distributing the vodka like, "Some for you and some for you …"

"What the fuck is a selfie?" said Miss Sheryl.

"When a stupid person with a smartphone flicks themselves and looks at it," I said to the room.

She replied with a raised eyebrow, "Oh?"

It's amazing how the news seems so instant to most from my generation—with our iPhones, Wi-Fi, tablets, and iPads—but actually it isn't. The idea of information being class-based as well became evident to me when I watched my friends talk about a weeks-old story as if it happened yesterday.

Miss Sheryl doesn't have a computer and definitely wouldn't know what a selfie is. Her cell runs on minutes and doesn't have a camera. Like many of us, she's too poor to participate in pop culture. She's on public assistance, lives in public housing, and scrambles for odd jobs to survive.

Sheryl lost her job as a cook moments after she lost her daughter to heroin, her son, Meaty, to crack, and her kidneys to soul food.

It took fifteen to twenty unanswered applications a week for over a year for her to realize that no company wants to employ a woman on dialysis. Sometimes Bucket-Head and I chip in and buy groceries for her and her grandson, Lil Kevin, who has severe lead-paint poisoning but was diagnosed late and is too old to receive a check.

Bucket-Head is a convicted felon but not really. He was charged with a crime that he didn't commit. I know this because my late cousin did the shooting, and our whole neighborhood watched. Bucket was in the wrong place at the wrong time, and as many know, we are products of a "no snitching" culture.

As a result, the only work Bucket can find after ten years of false imprisonment is that of a day laborer with the Mexicans who post up in front of 7-Eleven or as a freelance dishwasher. Bucket's no angel, but he's also not a felon and doesn't deserve to be excluded from pop culture any more than Miss Sheryl or Dontay, who represents the definition of redemption to me.

I placed our cups on the table and the bottle in the center. "Me and Miss Sheryl are gonna whip ass tonight—hurry up, Dontay!" I yelled.

Dontay cleans nonstop. Roaches sleeping in the fridge, roaches relay-racing out of the cabinets carrying cereal boxes, purchasing homes, building families, slipping through cracks for fun, and weaving in and out of death—Dontay bleaches them all. Dontay doesn't take handouts from us and won't go on government assistance. He couldn't contribute to the chips and vodka that week, so he's cleaned for Miss Sheryl and would clean for Miss Sheryl even if there were no chips and vodka.

"Boy, we ready to play the cards. Stop acting selfie and sit yo ass at the table!" yelled Miss Sheryl from another room. We all laugh. Miss Sheryl's rooms are separated by white sheets; they look like a soiled ghost at night when the wind blows. Her son, Meaty, stole and sold her doors years ago, and housing never replaced them.

Dontay joined us at the table. "Takin' forever, boy, wit dem big ass feet!" yelled a happy Bucket. Dontay was wearing my old shoes. They are 13s and busting at the seams but Dontay's a size 8 and his foot is digging through the side. His arms are chunked and wrapped in healed sores from years of drug abuse. He's eight years clean off of the hard stuff now, but I met him way back when I was thirteen, in his wild days.

He was huddled over his girlfriend in the alley behind my house. I watched moments before as she performed an abortion on herself with a twisted coat hanger. She screamed like the sirens we hear all day. I couldn't stop looking at her. He gazed, too, in and out of a nod and then signaled me for help. I joined them. Together we dragged her to Johns Hopkins Hospital, which was under a mile away. Blood scabbed and dried on my hands, Nikes, and hooping shorts; she lived until she ODd months later. I've been cool with Dontay ever since.

"Tryin' get dem roach eggs, tee-he, tee-he-he-he, gotta get the bleach on da roach eggs! Den dey won't come back!" Dontay explained as he sat at the table.

I dealt the first hand. Miss Sheryl reminded me to deal to the left. "Always deal to the left, boy; the rule don't change!" she said. She has the widest jaws in the history of wide and jaws, thicker than both of her bloated caramel arms, which are thigh-size. I collected the cards, reshuffled, and dealt to the left. And there we were—my job-hungry, unemployed old heads, and me, the overworked college professor.

College professor? Not the kind of professor that makes hundreds of thousands of dollars for teaching one class a year but a broke-ass adjunct who makes hundreds of dollars for teaching thousands of classes a year. The other day, I read an article about an adjunct who died in a homeless shelter, and I wasn't surprised; panhandlers make triple, and trust me, I've done the research, I should be looking for a corner to set up shop.

I have a little more than my friends but still feel their pain. My equation for survival is teaching at three colleges, substituting, and freelancing as a whatever—web designer, graphic designer, rap video director, wedding photographer, tutor. The proceeds from all of these various labors are swallowed by my mortgage, cigarettes, rail vodka, and ramen noodles. I used to eat only free-range organic shit, I used to live in Whole Foods, I used to drink top shelf—I used to be able to afford pop culture.

But long gone are the days when I pumped crack into the very neighborhood where we hold our card game. Eons since I had to stay up all night counting money until my fingers cramped. Since I had to lie on my back to kick my safe closed, and I wore and treated Gucci like Hanes and drove Mercedes CLs and gave X5 Beamers to my girlfriends—my good ole days.

Eventually the mass death of my close friends caused me to leave the drug game in search of a better life. Ten-plus years and three college degrees later, I'm back where I started, just like my card-playing friends: too poor to participate in pop culture. Too poor to give a fuck about a selfie or what Kanye said or Beyoncé's new album and the seventeen videos that came with it.

"Put me on that Obamacare when you can, college boy!" Sheryl says to me as I contemplate the number of books I can make out of my shitty hand. We all laugh. I am the only one in the room with the skill set to figure it out, but we all really see Obamacare as another bill, and from what I hear, the website is as broke as we are. We love Barack, Michelle, their lovely daughters, and his dog, Bo, as much as any African American family, but not like in 2008.

The Obama feeling in 2008 wasn't the same as the Obama feeling in 2014. Obama had us dream-chasing in 2008. My friends and I wanted him to be our dad and best friend and mentor and favorite uncle. Shit, I wanted to take selfies with him. He was a biracial swirl of black and white Jesus sent to deliver us. To bless people stuck under the slums like Sheryl, Bucket, Dontay, and me with jobs, access to the definition of words like "selfie," and—*real hope.*

But in 2014, it feels the same as Bush, or Clinton, or any other president. The rich are copping new boats, and we still are using the oven to heat up our houses in the winter, while eating our cereal with forks to preserve milk. America still feels like America, a place where you have to pay to play, any- and everywhere, even here at our broke-ass card game.

When 1 a.m. rolls around, we're faded, everyone but Miss Sheryl, that is, because dialysis prohibits her from drinking. My kidney pounds, and her 2008 Obama for Pres T-shirt stares back at me all stretched out of shape, making Barack look like Sinbad. No one knows who won because, really, we all lost.

Dontay is asleep, and I saw the roaches creeping back, and Bucket staggered out.

I looked at Miss Sheryl, "We could take a late night selfie now, but I swapped my iPhone for a Boost Mobile, $30 payment!"

She laughed and said, "Baby, what's a selfie again?"

My Neighborhood Revolution

Feed up time, homies! Line that ass up!" yelled Deion, sweating like Pat Ewing in the fourth quarter over that scraped charcoal grill by the gate. He had packed it with little wings, salty turkey franks, and saltier turkey burgers on a 90-plus degree day down in Bocek Park.

It's Sunday, so old heads like me throw on Under Armour mixed with Nike Dri-FIT and try to blend in with the high schoolers on the blacktop—the up-and-coming stars. For hours, we competitively throw crossovers, jump shots, and slurs at each other in fun and peace. I lost my second game and two's my max, so I hit the grill line.

"Yo, are these chicken or pigeon wings?" I asked.

"They from Aldi's, yo!" Deion proclaimed, referencing Baltimore's favorite discount supermarket chain.

We all laughed and said definitely pigeon. I threw three on my plate, snatched a Deer Park from the cooler, and found a spot in the shade. Dub rolled up on me looking all urgent and uneasy with smirked eyebrows and said, "Yo, yo, lemme rap to you right quick, D."

My wings and I hopped up and followed him toward the street. He's built like a six-burner Viking stove in work boots. I remember when he was ripped like a protein-powder model, but this food makes us all fat and sick.

"What you want, Dub? I'm trying to eat!"

He dug in his pocket and pulled out a folded letter.

"Yo, if you tell somebody, Ima kill you, in real life," he mumbled. Someone from the court asked if I was next, but I waved him off.

"Yo, you sick or something? What's going on?"

He told me that he had been talking on the phone with his daughter in North Carolina at least once a week. She had the bright idea of them exchanging letters and had even sent the first one.

"So what you want—me to help you write a letter?" I asked. "Isn't that personal?"

"Naw D. I want you to read it for me. I don't know what she talking about. Don't tell nobody man I swear!"

He looked down at his boots and kicked gravel. I wondered, how could a forty-five-year-old man not know how to read?

I first thought of Dexter Manley, the former Washington Redskins star who graduated high school, spent four years at Oklahoma State, and made it to the pros all while being illiterate. His talents allowed him to be robbed of his education.

In a way, Dub is like Manley. Before he landed his city job, way back before his prison bit, Dub was an enforcer, which is the guy who beat up the guys who owed the kingpin's money. Some debtors got dangled out of windows; others he'd run down until they were breathless and then grind the heel of his boot into their gum line. Reading wasn't a requirement for his job, and he made plenty of money, just like Manley.

We used to call his overhand right the sleeper because every dude that caught it went right to sleep, and Dub didn't believe in picks or choices. He knocked out young guys, teenagers, old heads, dope fiends, student athletes, street guys, rappers, and church boys.

"Walk me to the store, man," I said. He followed me up Madison and down Curley. "So do you want me to teach you how to read?"

He said no because he was too old, he'd gotten this far without reading, and his brain doesn't work that well anymore.

"I got love for you my brother, but your answer sounds like something that only a person who couldn't read would say! I'm not reading your letter unless you let me or someone else teach you. It'll be between us."

"Naw, man, I work and I'm out the street, yo. I just wanna know what her letta say and maybe get one back. I'll pay you, but I ain't learnin' readin', shit borin' anyway."

Reading is boring" is a phrase I've been hearing at the beginning of each semester from the freshmen at Coppin State University, where I teach English 101. I give them my soliloquy on why it was illegal for slaves to read and how easy it was for masters to control populations of people with limited thoughts—partially due to illiteracy. I usually say, "Being smart and developing complex thoughts without reading is like trying to get Schwarzenegger muscles without working out."

Then I assign books like *Decoded* by Jay Z, and *The Other Wes Moore* by Wes Moore. I also scour the Internet for articles that speak directly to them. I believe that everyone would enjoy reading if they had the right material. Obtaining that material would not only provide the foundation for the basic skills needed but also spark a greater interest in literature outside of the classroom.

As a kid, I was only introduced to books like *Tom Sawyer* and *Huckleberry Finn*—those books made me shun literature. Now I understand how great Mark Twain is, but my perspective was different when I was a kid. I came from a neighborhood with shootouts, dirt bikes, police raids, junkie fights, block parties, and hoop tournaments. Adventures happened every day, and Twain seemed corny to kids like us; fences weren't being whitewashed with paint, but sidewalks were being red-washed with blood, and we were in the mix.

I wasn't hooked on books until I read Sista Souljah's *The Coldest Winter Ever*, *Clockers* by Richard Price, and a few Sherman Alexie essays. Those books opened up my mind and led to me consuming more and more. My thoughts changed, I developed new ideas, and I was forever transformed. Within months, I went from a guy who solved problems by breaking a bottle over someone's forehead to using solution-based thinking when resolving—reading instantly civilized me. And if it can work for me, I believe it can work for anybody.

Dub and I spit sunflower seed shells out on the way back to the court. I stopped and read the letter to him after he asked for the ten-thousandth time. She closed with, "Thank you for the extra cash ☺ I can't believe I'm finally off to college. I love you. You'll always be a part of me and even though you weren't there in the beginning, I'm blessed to have you here now."

Dub paused and snatched the letter. He turned away and said, "Hol up D, I gotta go down here right quick yo. I'll see you on the court."

"Yo, are you crying?" I asked. "That's enough of a reason to learn! Right?"

He continued down Curley Street without a response.

For weeks after, I thought about Dub and his daughter, wondering what I could do. To date, I've written essays that have been read by thousands, but most of my friends in Baltimore—where only 7 percent of African American males in the eighth grade read on grade level—haven't clicked on one. This disgusting reality has advanced my focus.

Initially, I wanted to raise awareness on the ills affiliated with the modern black experience by telling stories straight from my neighborhood, and it's working because outsiders are responding to me and sharing their changes and updated perspectives through tweets and email; however, waiting for that influence to trickle down into my neighborhoods isn't enough.

I'm responsible for sharing the power of reading with as many low-income people as I can reach. Not being able to reach everyone does not exempt me from making a conscious effort to push literacy every day in the streets, online, and in the schools. I will do this by continuing to create material that is relatable to nontraditional readers and, more importantly, encouraging more people to write, so if my story doesn't resonate with a segment of readers, someone else's will.

I caught up with Dub at a '90s party a week ago. Most of the guys from the court in the summer were present in their old-school Cross Colours jeans and Kani sweats. Dub was fresh in Nautica, New Balance, and square frames just like when I met him back in the day.

"Yooooo, you look a fat ass Uncle Phil version of the Dub I knew in '96!" I yelled, giving him a pound and a hug.

The same bullshit pigeon wings were being served with chips, a Subway platter, and a bunch of alcohol. I pulled Dub to the side and said, "Yo, I'm still down on that reading thing we rapped about if you want, man. I'm in the *City Paper* on the positive tip, and you can't even check me out."

He inhaled four or five wings at a time and spit the bones out like shotgun shells.

"D congrats my homie, but I ain't got the time. I'ma save your write-up tho. I gotta second job now, so I'm sendin my baby girl more college money. She the smart one, and that's good enough for me!"

That was good enough for him but not for me. I know that literacy plays a key role in communication, and our failure to communicate is evident in the crowded jails, the trash pigeon wings we eat, the multiple police shootings, and the many racial divides in America in general. Dub's okay being one of the thirty-two million people in America who can't read, and I can't force him to because he's way bigger than I am. But I am going to do everything in my power to make reading cool and destroy that Dub mentality, which is so common in Baltimore and many other low-income areas across America.

The number of illiterate people in our country is criminal. The number of people who are aware of the literacy rate and choose to do nothing is even more criminal. Convincing people to read in a society where the primary use for books is decorations and drink coasters will be extremely difficult; however, I think we can do it if we work together collectively and just take it one word, one sentence, one paragraph, and one book at a time.

I once heard Sherman Alexie say, "Rich people who don't read are assholes and poor people who don't read are fucked!" He's right. So if we can help create readers and writers, thinkers will be birthed, people will be better communicators, social relations will enhance drastically, and our city will be a less violent place.

Crimes of the Art

In Central Booking, Young Moose only gets two calls a day. I am sitting in the adjunct office of Coppin State University on the phone with the twenty-one-year-old Baltimore street-rap phenomenon born Kevron Evans, using up one of those calls.

His girlfriend, Nicole Jones, a criminal justice major at Coppin, is with me. Moose is on the speakerphone. Currently, his song "Dumb Dumb" plays on Baltimore rap and R&B station 92Q. The video for his song "Posted" has received hundreds of thousands of hits on YouTube since it was first released in December of last year. Local rap impresario and former Def Jam A&R man Tony Austin has signed Young Moose to his label Austin Music Group.

Moose tells me he's been rapping since he was a child: "I started rapping when I was eight years old. My grandma died, and I made a song about it. I spit it to my father, and he said it's good, so I kept goin' with that."

In August 2014, after a crazy buzz over the previous few months, thanks to "Posted" and the release of his mixtape "O.T.M. 2" in June, Young Moose was scheduled, along with Lor Scoota, another up-and-coming Baltimore rapper, to perform with Lil Boosie at the Arena. Three days before the show, Detective Daniel T. Hersl arrested Moose in connection with a July 25 raid. A warrant was issued to Hersl because of Moose's videos, including "Posted" and another one titled, "It's In Me," along with the testimony of a cooperating witness, who said they purchased drugs at the residence on July 22.

Moose says the drugs they found weren't his. "Yes, I've broken the law before, but that's my past," he tells me. "I'm not a drug dealer. I make music that represents the people where I come from."

After posting bail the day of the show, he was immediately brought in on a probation charge again, stemming partly from music videos, which Moose's lawyer Richard Woods says were recorded long before Moose was on probation. A YouTube description for "Posted" notes that the video was uploaded on December 18, 2013.

The video for "Posted" depicts what goes on in any impoverished Baltimore neighborhood with the cinematic flair of hood flicks like *Paid in Full*. It's thoughtfully shot and executed and feels more like a short film than just another rap video. To many people, what Moose does isn't art at all, though; it's just evidence. Cops never fucked with David Simon while he was filming *The Wire*, and dudes who rock out at that rock club The Crown sing about drugs and addiction weekly, but Moose can't do the same? Martin Scorsese can, but Moose can't? Can you not be an artist if you've dealt heroin? If you're a felon? If you've owned guns? So now being black and from the ghetto bars you from artistic expression?

Young Moose was brought to me by a seventh grader named Nick whom I met while working at Friendship Academy, a charter school in the Canton area. "I'm telling you, Watkins," he said, "ask anybody from anywhere DDH, projects, new homes, Westside, or whatever! Moose! Moose is that! He better than Boosie, Jeezy, everybody! Moose dummy!"

I was excited to hear that he hailed from my side of town. I'm also from DDH—Down Da Hill, the eastside of Baltimore near Hopkins Hospital and composed of every block past Eager Street to where Highlandtown begins. A few underground acts, such as Widge, the Low Boyz, and the late Tom Tom and Lil Boonie, emerged from our section of the city but never with this much excitement.

I decided to gauge Moose's buzz with a class I was teaching.

"Who ya'll listening to? Music wise?" I asked a class full of middle schoolers.

They all answered, "O.T.M. 2, O.T.M. 2, O.T.M. 2!" I had to check Young Moose's mixtape, *Out the Mud 2*, released as a free download in June. I downloaded the tape at school and bumped it on my way home from work and was hooked. He was making references to neighborhoods that I know. Neighborhoods that I've been through, telling raw stories that are both native to Baltimoreans and universal.

Moose is heavily inspired by Lil Boosie, The Hot Boyz, and some other out-of-town acts, but he still maintains his 410 swag. He rocks Prada shoes and films on Monument Street. He's in Tru's and New Balance with designer belts posted on vacants and in between alleys spitting real raps while big-ass rats leap over his feet. Moose doesn't act like he's from any other place in the world but east Baltimore, and it bleeds through in every song.

It's the stories in these songs that represent the people where he came from that give Moose a much greater range than an ordinary street rapper. *The Wire* brilliantly displayed the balance between police, dealers, politicians, reporters, and junkies and how their worlds collide through the eyes of David Simon and Ed Burns. Moose comes with a fresh perspective from a completely different reality; however, he is equally brilliant and can capture the same world through a lens that has never been seen before. There aren't many writers coming from DDH, and that's evident when seeing the clueless response to his music.

Almost two months after the Lil Boosie show, which he was unable to play because of his arrest, Moose is still locked up.

"I look up to Boosie as a rapper, and that was a big night for me," he says of the timing of the raid. "The biggest in my career so far. I was fucked up because how they going to go let them take my shine like that? It really was really sick."

I asked Moose to tell me about his experience with Detective Hersl.

"He's a dirty cop, and he has a personal vendetta against me," Moose says. "He always lies on me, and I only pleaded guilty to my last charge because he locked up a friend who wasn't supposed to go to jail. I can't remember a time when I wasn't bein' harassed by him. He keep harassing me and even attacked my mother. She asked Hersl for a warrant during the raid, and he said 'You must be Moose's mother, I have something better!' and then locked her up."

Detective Hersl has cost the city nearly $200,000 in police brutality and misconduct lawsuits, and yet he's still working the streets. Two hundred thousand dollars in settlements—all paid for by taxpayers like me. We pay his salary, we pay for his fuck-ups—and even after he breaks the law and does a horrible job, he is still free and employed. Moose, on the other hand, is now a law-abiding citizen and an entrepreneur, stimulating the local art community by producing and hiring locally. His only crime is his art.

Moose is a gifted storyteller who can deliver the human side of our Baltimore to the world. His music, in representing the people where he comes from, is authentic. It does not mean that it is a documentary or should be used as evidence. Those in power are most comfortable when they can ignore the poor and underrepresented—and they don't want artists like Moose to give these people a voice. But you can't shut up somebody like Young Moose by throwing him in jail.

"I just focus on life, real life," he tells me. "It's my gift." All those who value it have to make sure he goes free, and stays free.

Chasin' the Gram

The English 101 class I teach at Coppin State University is the shit. Technology is on point, we have the latest everything, and my students are amazing.

I assign hot contemporary books—right now we're reading Jay Z's *Decoded*. We also read multiple essays by both Junot Diaz and Sherman Alexie in addition to the books that the college recommends. My students and I rep the same generation—I look like them, we're close in age, and we even bump the same music. So why can't they focus in class?

Why do 20 to 30 percent of them get lost midway through our discussions? Our topics are relevant and normally centered around critical thinking, transformative arcs, and universal truths, and often cause heated arguments over subjects they care about—or at least subjects that they tell me they care about. I ask because I really care. And they engage for a while, but then they proceed to scroll.

They scroll. Their heads tilt and dip like the methadone fiends in front of Lexington Market, their eyes locked on Instagram as they finger their smartphones for the remainder of class and even after it has ended, to the point where I have to yell, "Y'all can leave now! Get out!"

They spend hours aimlessly scrolling, absorbing fake and altered realities, praising the lives of celebrities when they could be enjoying real life, participating in rich discussions, and learning. I can't blame the "boring" stigma usually attached to English 101 because our class is fun, and I won't write my students off as lazy.

Something has to change, I thought. I beat the streets, I've never been to prison, I survived east Baltimore's semi-automatic-weapon crack era, I figured out how to learn in public schools, and I escaped murder multiple times, so I know I can beat a free iPhone app. My lessons are interesting, and the idea of Instagram beating me sounds ridiculous.

So I decided to slap my class with a high-energy rant on why their addiction to social media is toxic, robbing them of real life experiences, making them robots. For about fifteen minutes, I ripped and fulminated against checking timelines during class. My arms swung back and forth like a conductor, spit flung from my mouth and drenched the students in the front row, and all of the cell phones were tucked away. Everyone sat erect, and some even cheered me on. I made my point, and I finally got through to 100 percent of my students!

Well 99 percent, because someone Instagrammed a clip of my lecture with the caption, "This nigga crazy!"

But I didn't feel completely defeated. I know I reached someone: Tyree, a stocky freshman football player who witnessed that rant from the back row, approached me after class.

"I gotta apologize to you in advance," he said gripping his phone, looking down at his feet.

"Why Tyree? What's wrong?"

Tyree picked up his chin and tightened his neck. His shoulders were as wide as my desk. I repeated my question. "What's wrong man?"

His eyes welled up. "I can't sit in class for a hour without checking my IG, and I know you said it's making me fail, but I can't do it!"

He went to tell me that he IGs or "chases the Gram" before he goes to sleep, when he wakes up, and when he drives.

"You IG and drive, Tyree! Are you crazy?" I said, shocked that he's willing to die over filtered pictures. I pulled up a chair and sat him down.

Together, we analyzed his timeline. I had to see what he saw. I had to figure out why he would let this app threaten his safety. We scrolled. He follows thousands of people with posts that are about as unique as a person in skinny jeans and dark frames nowadays. Multiple selfies, party-promoter fliers, big booty girls who were hacked at 200k, and pictures of food—disgusting food, like trays of white macaroni with eight pieces of American cheese laying across the top, impatiently waiting to be melted, with a caption that reads something like, "My grandma makes the best mac and cheese." And then more pics of the same stuff on repeat, over and over again, each photo more underwhelming than the next.

"You'll be a fool if you fail because of IG, Tyree, but risking your life is crazy! I can't believe you look at face pics and dull food shots while driving! Does Instagram send you checks? You know you are paying for your education? Think about it."

I wanted to slap him. I really wanted to confiscate his phone like a drunk driver's keys; he's just as dangerous. Tyree left in shame, and I was beyond pissed. I wasn't sure if it was because he was so willing to accept defeat or because I was off work and he cut into my IG time.

Yes, I'm addicted, too. And I didn't realize it until my own rant made me think about checking my page.

I'd never check my page while teaching or driving, but I definitely check it while I'm doing everything else—drinking, eating, sleeping, cleaning. I checked it 230 times while writing this article (I counted).

I check my Instagram as much as my students, if not more. My skin itches, and I become physically ill when away from my timeline for too long. I care about my likes, too. I monitor my followers, and I hopelessly double-tap ridiculous pictures that I don't really like with hopes of the ridiculous picture-poster returning the favor and making me equally ridiculous.

Instagram is an escape for me, too. There are more dangerous escapes out there, such as heroin, but well . . . let me retract that, IG is our dope, which would probably make Facebook methadone.

And it's not a white thing or a black thing; it's an addict thing. Neither I nor a student like Tyree is any different from the rich white kid at Harvard who chases the Gram in between yacht parties and games of polo—the Gram distracts us all. The only difference between that rich white kid and Tyree is that the rich white kid is a rich white kid, meaning that he can afford to fuck up. He has a backing, and unlike Tyree, who is a first-generation college student, failing English 101 will not stop his financial aid and get him kicked out of school.

Street kids from Baltimore like Tyree can't afford to fail classes, especially English, in a city where only 7 percent of African American males in the eighth grade read on grade level. We need to save every kid who's willing to come to class. So, maybe, as parents and educators, we can change the way we look at this whole social media thing.

If we all know that these kids are going to be in the same place at the same time with their eyes locked on the same social networks, then why can't we find a way to reach them there and educate them? Why can't we use social media as a tool to guide the lost children back into the schools while connecting with and enlightening them on levels unimaginable without social media?

I'm sure that I'm not the first one to pose this idea, but perhaps I can play role in making the shift.

When the end of the semester rolled around, Tyree, a great kid with the potential to earn As and Bs, showed some growth as a writer, but he ended up with a C. IG distractions hindered his potential. Monitoring the effects that the Gram had on a student like Tyree has led me to question my own growth and to wonder what I could accomplish if I didn't punch that app so much.

So, I deleted it with the hopes of being more productive.

But then downloaded it again a few hours later.

What to Eat?

Lemon Heads, Now and Laters, Flamin' Hot Cheetos, BBQ sunflower seeds, Boston Baked Beans, penny candies of every flavor, butterscotch cookies, butterscotch Krimpets, Twinkies, Twix, Takis, and M&Ms; that's the menu my friends and I shared every morning on the way to elementary, middle, and high school—and the reason we all have meth-mouth-looking teeth with chopped up incisors and rotten molars.

I'm sure there are probably millions of other city kids who start their day with the same diet the same way. Loads of sugar and some yellow dye #5 mixed with a bunch of other unpronounceable chemicals all conjoined and neatly packaged in eye-catching wrapping paper. Kids with money eat the same thing for lunch while others are forced to eat the meals provided by the school, which wasn't much better in my day. And then there's soul food, microwavable poison, or Mickey D's for dinner.

I don't remember anyone addressing how dangerous food could be to me as a kid back in the '90s and early 2000s. Carryout spots like Moe's in downtown Baltimore that sold fat-fried, jumbo crab cakes catered my early teens when I thought I knew what good food was. My side items would be a biscuit, mashed potatoes, and a pile of vegetables that floated in warm butter, which I never ate.

Skipping vegetables was easy for me, and, honestly, I don't know how I got to be so tall without them. But eating them probably wouldn't have done much for my body—how healthy can overcooked greens soaked in pork fat be?

I never cared about my diet until I became a full-time crack dealer. It woke me up, just sitting outside seeing a lot of the older dudes and junkies who hung around my block looking all worn out. I expected that physical decay from the drug addicts but not from the regular guys who really didn't drink and were only two or three years older than I was. Slim dudes maintained their skinny legs but grew bubble guts, pie faces, and small perky breasts. The women weren't any better. The prettiest girls doubled in size like the Hulk. They became big-bodied with little tiny heads like chickens. OG Ron was one of the more fit dudes in the hood. You know, that shirtless dude with the long cornbraids doing pull-ups in the park—he schooled me first like, "Shorty, I learned all about that fast food in da joint! Cook your own shit, or get your lady to cook ya food. Like real stuff, not that corner store shit they passin' off as food!"

At the time I had an eight-pack of abs like him, and I was trying to keep them, but I wasn't cooking dinner, and there were no young women in my dating pool who were dedicated to making me three hots a day. I didn't go looking for a chef; I just switched from chicken boxes with salt, pepper, and ketchup to Subway sandwiches—they helped that fat guy in the commercial lose 300 pounds, and the subs sure looked healthier than the crap I was eating. But then I met Miss Angie, and just in time, too, because the sandwiches started tasting like shit.

My friends and I had been building a crack strip on Maderia Street right off of Ashland Avenue on the eastside of Baltimore. Miss Angie wasn't really a part of our crew, but she was. She'd been living on Maderia Street for a thousand years, and she'd seen a bunch of crews before us and would probably see a bunch of crews after us.

I took a liking to her because she was a hustler just like me, just like us. She'd tell us dope-boys all about her church and Jesus and then say, "Buy one of my fresh chicken dinners, baby, they only $8!" Slanging crack all day definitely builds up an appetite, and her dinners were actually delicious. Her house was beige in the inside and smelled like old people mixed with mothballs. She had canned goods stacked up to the ceiling, and the only fruit was plastic and piled in a dusty centerpiece on her kitchen table. Miss Angie had a big picture of white Jesus on her wall. I kept telling her Jesus was black, but she didn't listen.

"If Jesus was black, then why he white on all these pictures, D! Riddle me that!" she'd say.

"Cuz white people want you to associate them with God. That nigga was black, I'm tellin' you! Hair like wool! That's a Jeri Curl!" I'd tell her, then we'd share a laugh.

Eventually, I ignored the painting because her cooking was better than eating the carry trash and plastic Subway sandwiches every day, plus she always made a vegetable. OG Ron had beat, "You gotta eat vegetables errry day to not be like deeez fat ass niggas!" into my head, so I had to make sure I got my veggies. And even though her vegetables were always smothered in pig parts and butter like Moe's, we weren't getting them from anywhere else, so I had to deal.

The best part about Miss Angie was her hours. As long as I kept cash in her purse and food in her fridge, I could get a hot meal at any time of the day. It could be 3 or 4 a.m., after the after hour, and all I had to do was knock. She'd hop up and start frying, baking, and microwaving shit. I'd kick back and light a blunt. By the time I was finished smoking, I'd have a five-star hood meal waiting.

This lasted a year or so, and as I progressed by stepping outside of my east Baltimore neighborhood, I learned that the hormone-filled chicken and canned vegetables from Miss Angie weren't good for me, just like the Subway sandwiches with those genetically modified vegetables and fresh-baked bread that contains the same foaming agent found in yoga mats. That put me right back into the same situation: not knowing what to eat. And I'm not alone—African Americans have struggled with the same problem ever since we were shipped to this country.

Poor eating habits have been plaguing the black community since the days of slavery, when captured Africans were given scraps, filth, and unpronounceable parts of the pig for breakfast, lunch, and dinner. Every once in a while, a slick slave would hit a chicken or pig over the head with a rock and then present it to the overseer as being defective so they could have a nice meal, but the norm was guts, gizzards, and hog ass.

The tradition of unhealthy eating seems be unshakable in the black community and becomes evident when considering that the risk of diabetes is 77 percent higher among African Americans than among non-Hispanic white Americans. The stats jump off the page as I walk down the streets of the neighborhoods where I grew up or even Miss Angie's old block and see new generations of overweight people, some younger than me with missing limbs and chopped off toes. What bothers me the most is that we know the effects of our eating and don't aggressively seek change.

I once watched a movie called *Soul Food* in which a matriarchal grandma named Big Mama had her family over to her house for huge soul food dinners every week. She'd serve fried everything, from fish to string beans, yams extra syrup, different types of cornbread, and diabetes-flavored tea, and topped the meal off with cake and ice cream for everyone. Eventually, her diet caused her to have a massive heart attack. As a result, she had her leg chopped off, and then she died. The family suffered a tremendous amount of pain and broke apart because of the death but eventually found a way to reunite by cooking and eating the same food that killed Big Mama. Everybody knew the result and still chose to do the same thing.

I'm extremely happy that Michelle Obama, along with some other prominent public figures, has made a conscious effort to tackle our food problem and stress the importance of good diet and exercise—but it still feels like the message isn't fully resonating with my community.

What is it going to take for us to eat right? The fear of disease and premature death clearly isn't working. We are marching and protesting against police brutality, but biscuits and gravy and macaroni and cheese are probably killing us at a more alarming rate.

SIDE TWO

Fuck the National Anthem

I hit a basketball game the other day. Hundreds packed into the stands and around the court as the DJ silenced the music. A bouncy, colorful dude approached center-court and requested that we stand for the national anthem. A delicate teenage Whitney Houston type approached the mic.

Everyone popped up, blacks and whites alike, all with straight backs and erect necks, their right palms Velcroed to their hearts. Military silence blanketed the crowd as the little girl blessed us all with her voice.

I stayed seated and just played on my iPhone during her entire performance. Some people looked at me, I yawned in their direction, stretched in my seat, and looked back at them. I was itching for someone to say something stupid like, "Pay some respect. Stand for the anthem" so I could've broke my mug down and yelled, "Man, fuck you and the anthem!"

I would've proudly hollered that at the top of my lungs because obviously I don't fit the mold. Even though I was born in America, and my ancestors built its infrastructure for free, I'm not a part of the "Our" when they sing, "Our flag was still there!" I feel like the "Our" doesn't include blacks, most women, gays, trans, and poor people of all colors.

And, sadly, our nation reminds us every day.

Some may reject the anthem because Francis Scott Key sang for freedom while enslaving blacks. His hatred even bled into the lyrics of the elongated version of "The Star-Spangled Banner" you won't hear at a sporting event. The third stanza reads:

No refuge could save the hireling and slave/From the terror of flight, or the gloom of the grave

That line was basically a shot at slaves who agreed to fight with the British during the War of 1812 in exchange for their freedom. Who wouldn't want freedom, and how could Key not understand someone in shackles opting for a better life? A life free of whippings, rape, and unpaid labor.

Andrew Jackson caught wind of slaves agreeing to fight with the British in exchange for freedom and made a similar promise to thousands of slaves in Louisiana. He told them if they protected Louisiana from the redcoat invaders, they could be free after the war. Well, we won the war, and then Jackson reneged on the deal. He went on to be president while the brave Africans who fought with honor went back into servitude.

Others reject our national anthem for more contemporary reasons, pointing to generation after generation of broken promises. It's two hundred years later, and America still enslaves a tremendous amount of its population through poverty, lack of opportunity, false hopes of social mobility, unfair educational practices, and the prison-industrial complex.

I've long been aware of how our nation treats its minorities and the underclass, but despite everything, I still gave America the benefit of the doubt. After all, we have a black president right?

Obama gave me super hope back in '08, but then reality set in. I get that the change I'd like to see is probably going to take hundreds of years of reform. But I wasn't expecting the first black president to kill more people with drones and lock up more whistleblowers than his disastrous predecessor, George W. Bush, while furthering the militarization of our country. Despite all of that, I still wanted to keep the faith with Obama's America. I tried to give our nation credit for the progress we've made in race relations, but fuck it, then Ferguson happened. It was the last straw.

Eighteen-year-old Mike Brown was gunned down by Ferguson, Missouri, police officer Darren Wilson for no reason other than the color of his skin. Wilson shot him down as if he was inhuman and did not deserve freedom or the right to live, like the slaves Francis Scott Key wrote about two hundred years before. To top that, Wilson left the young man's dead body on the sizzling concrete in the dead of summer for four hours.

Darren Wilson, the coward who performed this heinous act, was given a pass by the state and local authorities and allowed to walk free. It was just the latest in a long, long line of outrages and abuses stretching all the way back to the beginning of this country.

This is the same country that jailed Michael Vick two years for killing dogs and let George Zimmerman walk after using an inno-cent black teen for target practice. The same culture that simply shrugged off the shootings of Sean Bell and Amadou Diallo with a straight face. They "Radio Raheem"-ed Eric Garner, too. Beating Rodney King was legal at one point, right?

America has become a place that makes up a bullshit sickness like "affluenza" to exonerate rich white murderers, while stuffing the prisons full of young black men on petty charges. We're the home of

Jim Crow, the Trail of Tears, community lynchings. Remember the Jena 6? America did the Scottsboro Boys dirty, too. They smashed Lil' Bobby Hutton, right? They popped King, they popped Malcolm, they popped Medgar, and they popped Fred Hampton in his bed. Now that there are no more black leaders to kill, they are popping kids like Mike Brown.

If young Michael Brown had been white, he would be taking English 101, posting selfies, or doing homework for some philosophy class right now. Instead, he has joined a mile-long list of unarmed black teens who were murdered by remorseless, badge-wearing, bloodthirsty police officers who identify as patriots and obviously have no regard for black life.

I refuse to salute a flag or honor a song promoted by a country that allows these tragedies to happen over and over again. Fuck a pointless statement from some politician, and double-fuck anyone who would ever fire a rubber bullet at a peaceful protester.

I'm a teacher, and all of my students look like Mike Brown, or Jonathan Farrell, or Ramarley Graham, or Renisha McBride, or Aiyana Jones, or Trayvon Martin, or Tyisha Miller, or Kathryn Johnson, or Tarika Wilson, or Oscar Grant, or Yvette Smith, or John Crawford. What should I tell them?

Should I tell my students that these incidents were mistakes so they won't be scared to leave their homes? Or should I be honest and say that according to *The Washington Post*, 313 black people (many of whom were unarmed) were murdered by the police in 2012—that's one black life every twenty-eight hours. I choose the latter.

I tell them to document the police in their neighborhoods with their camera phones because bloodthirsty cowards like Darren Wilson have closets full of guns and are eager to use them on innocent people that look just like you. And then I tell them Darren Wilson doesn't represent all white people or cops in general, but there are many active officers just like him. I also tell them that we are not perfect, and our country is not perfect, but we can change if we want to.

America has enough power and influence to strengthen race relations; however, at this particular time in history, our country is not trying hard enough. "The Star-Spangled Banner" is not for people like us. The "rockets' red glare" just makes me think of the drone strikes in Pakistan and Yemen or the police firepower at home. So for now, I'm sitting out the anthem.

Cops Kill Blacks in America

I'm sitting in the car directly across from Latrobe Housing Projects in Baltimore's Old Town district. Some teenagers in Polo are posted by the corner store. There's a game of football going on by the court-yard. Tackle on concrete, with clothesline poles representing first downs and end zones. The same way we used to play back in the day, the reason why our bones and teeth are chipped up now.

I wanted to walk over for a closer look but I couldn't. I was pulled over as always. Doesn't matter what I drive. I've pushed every-thing from showroom clean BMW 750s to tight ass Honda Civics I could hardly fit in, and the result is always the same—some buzz-cut white boy eyes me doing twenty-nine in thirty, spots me wearing my seatbelt, and instantly thinks that I'm transporting nuclear weapons and bricks of heroin for the Taliban.

They have to stop me and my terrorist agenda, but they can't do it alone, so they call for back-up and then get back-up for their back-up.

Red and blue flashing lights were knocking against my rear-view mirror and blinking on my cell as I scrolled through text. Red, white, and blue is supposed to mean freedom right? Not if you are black—and *never* in this situation.

Knocks on my window . . .

This cop doesn't have a buzz cut at all—he kind of looks like the dad from *The Wonder Years* but whiter and more wrinkled. He's built like a jar of mayonnaise and walks like one, too.

"Do you know why I stopped you?" his face jiggles.

"Naw."

"Gimme your license and registration!"

"I'm . . . slowly . . . going . . . into . . . my . . . glove box . . . to . . . grab . . . them."

Moving fast or showing too much emotion is the quickest way to turn a routine traffic stop into a tragedy. If an officer even almost thinks you're reaching for a gun, they'll pump you with a hundred-plus shots like Amadou Diallo and Sean Bell—two working guys like me, who were profiled and then executed just because.

Officer Mayo takes my license and walks back to his car. This is some bullshit, I think. It wasn't always like this.

Back in the day we had Officer Friendly, a cop that came into our schools and greeted us with love and respect. Now our neighborhoods are full of racist cops who just harass, plunder and kill.

Knocks on my window . . .

"Step out of the car, son, let me search it, and I'll let you go!" he says with a raised eyebrow.

"Fuck outta here, son. That's not gonna happen—what's wrong with my paperwork?"

"Nothing, it checked out, but you are in a Target Drug Zone. Step out, let me look around, and we'll make this quick."

"That's not gonna happen, Slim."

Officer Mayo reddens up to a hint past tomato. He vomits anger into his radio as he waddles back to his car squeezing my license and registration. Maybe I should let him check it, I'm clean, and I hate waiting, but fuck that, these assholes get away with too much. I can't help but think about kids like Jonathan Ferrell as I wait. He was that twenty-four-year-old kid from North Carolina who took ten shots because he needed help from a cop.

Ferrell wrecked his car and knocked on a woman's door for help—he was black in America so she called the police. A racist cop quickly arrived on the scene and helped himself to a young black target. He probably salivated at the notion of killing a black kid, probably dreaming about the awards, medals, and Zimmerman love he'd receive as he aimed and squeezed.

That kid Ferrell was close to my age, looked like he could've been one of my friends. We are from the same country that is governed by the same bullshit, meaning that the same thing could happen to me as well and the reason why African Americans do not call the police for anything—ever.

Well, we do call when we need police reports for insurance purposes, but that's it.

Now two other cop cars have pulled up, blocking traffic in different directions. Two younger versions of Officer Mayo pop out and also a thin token black one, the Uncle Tom wildcard, a.k.a. "The Aggressor."

"What the fuck is going on!" yells the black one. He looks Republican; maybe he was that one black Tea Party member. The token paces, back and forth like a dumbass—I bury my head deep into the steering wheel. That was the safest place, I didn't have a gun on me to match their weaponry and exiting my car would leave me like Ferrell or Bell or Diallo or Martin or . . . you can fill in the latest black victim here.

"Get ya ass out of the car! What are you hiding? You know where you are at?" yells the black one. His eyes are bugged—poking out.

"I'm a teacher, and I'm in east Baltimore," I say, remaining as calm and as patient as Mumia. That's right—a teacher, so why fuck with me? I'm a student and a teacher in one of the most dangerous and illiterate places in the United States, meaning that I pose a threat to nothing but my liver. My tax dollars from the small amount of money I receive pay them to fuck me over.

Why was I sitting there for nothing? I had seen three drug transactions in the last eight minutes, under the flashing blue police lights—but I'm the bad guy. Diallo the cab driver was the bad guy, Sean Bell the newlywed was the bad guy, and Jonathan Ferrell the college football player was the bad guy.

Another inconvenient ten or fifteen minutes go by. I watch them talk and joke as I sit. Mayo approaches my car.

"You have a light out, and here's a repair order. Stay outta this neighborhood!"

I laugh. My light isn't out. They are just being assholes because I know my rights and pose no threat. I was lucky; they could've planted drugs on me, which the BCPD is famous for, or left me like Bell or Diallo or Martin or Ferrell.

I recently read that Randall Kerrick, the cop who shot Ferrell, was charged with voluntary manslaughter—which means he could do up to twenty years in prison. He'll probably be paroled in three. Is that justice? Would this system show Ferrell the same love if he had shot Kerrick? The answer is FUCK NO; he'd probably get the hot seat in this lopsided justice system that enslaves and kills black people daily.

On the brighter side, Kerrick will do some jail time unlike the devil George Zimmerman, who just sold a bullshit painting on eBay for $100K.

I hope Randall Kerrick thinks about Jonathan Ferrell every day during his sentence, from the crack of dawn until lights out. I hope his cell buddy is black, aware of the case, and beats him senselessly until he hides in PC. I hope the COs in PC are black and beat him until general population is his only option. I hope he finds out that his wife remarried a black guy named Travon or Jamal when he exits PC. And then I hope he feels the same depression that he delivered to the Ferrell family, asking himself the same question every day: *Why did I rob that kid of his life?*

And then I hope he does the only honorable thing he could and should do. Honor Ferrell's family by killing himself.

But that wont happen. Kerrick will exit prison and reunite with his family. He'll get a job and easily be accepted back into society. He'll enjoy Christmas', Easter's and Thanksgivings. He'll probably take corny Carnival cruise ship vacations over the summer. He'll sit at the buffet by the water and talk to strangers about family, love and maybe his days as a cop. Kerrick will get to enjoy the rest of his life. He'll completely forget about Jonathan Ferrell.

We won't.

RIP Jonathan Ferrell. Shit, RIP to them all.

Postscript: *I'm sad to say I was right. Kerrick was sentenced around the time I wrote this essay. In 2015, he appealed and it ended in a mistrial. Prosecutors won't seek retrial, allowing Kerrick to join the long list of cops that murdered innocent Black people and got away.*

Black Lives Do
Matter . . . to Capitalists

The dot-com bubble was great for America, right? Mark Cuban along with a bunch of other smart people made fortunes. And what about the housing bubble? Scores of ambitious American speculators flooded their bank accounts before the racket exploded back in 2008—and they all passed Go without going to Jail.

Lately I've been obsessing over these historic times in our nation's economy and impatiently wondering what's next. Where's the next boom coming from, or can there even be another boom in these rough economic times?

I researched countless theories, read tons of money magazines, and scoured the Internet for savvy trends before a CNN update on Ferguson, Missouri, clearly identified the next bubble. Our country's next big, get-rich-quick boom? The Kill-an-Unarmed-Black-Teen Bubble.

The news update briefly shed light on the huge amounts of money Darren Wilson and George Zimmerman received after murdering innocent black children. Neighborhood security watchman and Florida native Zimmerman raised hundreds of thousands of dollars on his personal website after murdering Trayvon Martin, an unarmed child making a routine trip to the store for Skittles. I'm from Baltimore city where people beat murder charges for $5K all of the time, so I'm not sure why Zimmerman needed hundreds of thousands. The world watched, and the case brought him instant celebrity status. After his acquittal, Zimmerman hit the interview circuit, where he tried to run the price up on Barbara Walters for an up-close exclusive while collecting checks from other networks. Meanwhile, he blew $3,600 on a luxury two-night hotel stay, where he took multiple trips to the spa and splurged on a dinner for ten. Where else in the world can a volunteer security guard murder an unarmed child and be rewarded with a luxury hotel stay? Now Zimmerman gets paid to do appearances and sign autographs as a special guest at gun shows, sold the gun he murdered Martin for six figures and made money of his bullshit artwork.

Police officer Darren Wilson, the murderer of the unarmed eighteen-year-old Michael Brown, was reportedly paid six figures to tell his side of the story to ABC News (ABC denies paying Wilson). However, we do know that he has earned enough to resign from the Ferguson Police Department. On top of the TV money accusations, the *Los Angeles Times* reported that two GoFundMe pages collectively raised over $400k on behalf of Wilson, who didn't even need a fundraiser. All of Wilson's legal fees were covered by the police union, so maybe he gets to keep all of those donations to enjoy, you know, life.

Yes, both of these men were able to gain small fortunes without any traces of intelligence or real talent. But don't be fooled, the Kill-an-Unarmed-Black-Teen Bubble isn't for everyone. Allow me to list the criteria.

To qualify, you have to be . . .

1) White or white/Hispanic
2) A police officer or security guard . . . or (see above) just a white guy
3) Heartless
4) And most important, your victim must be an unarmed black man (preferably underage). If you shoot a white teen, you can possibly go to jail.

Now, as a black man with a heart who probably couldn't qualify to be an officer and wouldn't shoot anyone, I don't meet any of the criteria; however, a large segment of America does. And there's no reason why some enterprising, young white man in middle America shouldn't have seen the same CNN report, and instantly ripped the American flag off of the wall in his mom's basement and used it to polish his pistol and shine up his rifle. Time to go hunting! Of course, all the better for the ambitious young man if he's also training to be a police officer or moonlights as a neighborhood watchman.

Through our broken legal system and our deranged media circus, men like Wilson and Zimmerman have found a way to profit off of black lives. They aren't the first, and they probably won't be the last.

Black Cop Down

Twenty-eight hours had passed. I know this because another unarmed black person was murdered in America by another racist, trigger-happy police officer—or so I thought when the Los Angeles Skid Row video was released in March 2015. But I was wrong; this time it wasn't the usual story of an unhinged white cop mistaking a student for a criminal. It was actually a group of cops beating, and then the black cop murdering, an unarmed Cameroonian immigrant known to his friends as "Africa."

A black cop murdering a black guy named Africa, in one of the most racially charged climates of our country's history. Was he blind, crazy? Did his TV not work?

I couldn't believe my eyes. Enraged, I reran the clip three times, thinking about the victim's family and friends, before I had to stop and realize that this is nothing new. It's business as usual. There weren't many black cops patrolling my east Baltimore neighborhood back when I was coming up; however, the few present in the eastern district were just as bad as the racist white cops, if not worse.

None of the black cops who used to run us down and beat on us back in the day were from our neighborhood, but I'd bet that they were from some densely black area and well aware of our history in dealing with police in general.

I guess they put something in the water at the police academy, something that transforms everyday African Americans looking for jobs into super asshole cops that harass and power trip in the same manner as their white counterparts. The attitudes of all of these dudes had my friends and me never-ever wanting to be cops—and the system made sure most of us wouldn't qualify by the time we finished high school anyway. The first guy I knew from the city who actually went through with being a cop was Dax.

Dax stood clear when we stomped down the wide hallways of Dunbar High. He'd walk away when fights broke out and hid behind his earphones when we slung plastic trays and half-full milk cartons across the cafeteria.

Dax stood about 5 foot nothing and was slim in the body with droopy eyes and a peanut-shaped head. He wasn't bullied because he was kinda cool. That dude never cracked slick, always rocked a sweater, and was the unofficial leader of our high school's Friend Zone, meaning that every girl from ninth to twelfth grade was responsible for giving him a hug before homeroom, meaning he could put in a good word for you with anyone you crushed on, meaning that giving him a rough time could guarantee that you'd be left dateless for your whole high school career. So yeah, he was cool.

Dax was two grades over me, and we lost touch shortly after he graduated. I didn't see him for four or five years, until we crossed paths in front of a nightclub in downtown Baltimore. Some friends and I were walking in as he spotted me and pulled me to the side. By then, he was on the force, but it sure didn't seem like he was there to serve and protect.

"D, wuddup nigga it's been a minute, I ain't going in this bitch ass club without both of my guns!" he yelled, pulling up his T-shirt to show me and the crowd the weapon stuck in his waistline. "I ain't playin wit' these bitch ass niggas out cheah, you feel me?"

I eyed him like a tough equation, said, "Have a good night," and got the hell away from him. Later that week, I brought up our little exchange at the basketball court with some other dudes we went to school with, and the nightmare stories flooded from every direction. Dudes chimed in calling him a clown that whips out his gun all crazy, pulls girls over and gives them tickets when they won't date him, picks random fights, pops shit on a regular, and partners with coworkers when dancing on the skulls of black teens.

My homie Tavon, a year under me at Dunbar High, said, "Oh you ain't know? Dax will fuck your whole shit up; he'll really rearrange your face. He ain't black no more, he's white! Better yet he's blue, he's with the biggest gang in the city!"

"The biggest gang in the city," I echoed, stepping back and throwing up a jump shot. The quote stuck with me for years after I first heard it, and it still does. Color doesn't matter when dealing with the police department; they only care about class and power.

If you're white, chances are you won't be shot during a routine traffic stop or even pulled over for a routine traffic stop. If you're black and rich, they'll stop you, then you might get a pass or a ticket, but you won't be murdered. Every other black person is fucked, and it doesn't matter if you are a man or a woman, they'll kill you dead.

You don't even have to be guilty and they'll kill you dead, and what makes matters worse is that our system expects us to follow laws and be honest while these cops will lie, steal, cheat, and do anything to protect their fellow gang members—like the fictitious story created by Michael Slager, the South Carolina killer cop, and corroborated by his black partner, Officer Clarence Habersham, in the shooting of Walter Scott—yet another Unarmed Black Man.

When Slager pulled Walter Scott over, Scott ran, apparently scared that he would be jailed for falling behind on his child support payments. Scott was a victim of a system that criminalizes debt, that penalizes poverty. He had been jailed three times before for being delinquent on his child support—losing his dream job in the process and falling into a spiral of deepening despair. He was finally beginning to climb out when Officer Slager pulled him to the curb. As Scott sprinted for freedom—away from the deep hole that threatened to pull him back down—a frustrated Slager drew his gun and shot him in the back, for no real reason, just because he could. Slager then walked next to the corpse and tossed his stun gun to the ground. His plan was to lie and say that he feared for his life because Scott took his Taser. And Habersham was right there with him. This African American lawman willingly backed up his fellow cop with a pack of lies that he called a police report, leaving me to think that these clowns must do this all the time. What's worse is that Slager was caught on tape laughing about the incident shortly after the murder. And by the time our community learns the ins and outs of vicious murders like the Scott case, we click our TVs on, and another one happens. I hope these cases make us all pay more attention to systemic racism.

Firing Dax, the black cop who murdered Africa, the black cop who lied in the case of Walter Scott, and the three black cops who assisted in the murder of Freddie Gray will not change the problem with our police departments. They are all just small, disposable pawns that are part of a system that produces thousands of officers just like them all over the country every year. The cop can be white, black, Asian, Latino, or a mix of them all; it doesn't matter, because they are all instantly groomed to perfectly fit into the classic old-boy-slave-catcher culture that has been in place for hundreds of years. The culture that makes cops of color show immense restraint when dealing with whites and brutal force when dealing with African Americans is that same culture from which they draw a salary, benefits, and retirement.

I wish my friends and I weren't so jaded by the police department. If more African Americans joined the police force, then maybe they wouldn't be so quick to take the side of their white brothers when they gunned down a defenseless black man. Maybe they could protect black communities instead of terrorizing them. That's all wishful thinking—but as it is now, the black cops enforce just like the racist white ones, and I fear that the story of Africa of Skid Row or Walter Scott or Freddie Gray will not be the last time I get disgusted by horror stories involving black cops.

Cops Are the Terrorists in Our Neighborhood

G D is a high-energy guy, always turned to max. Happy or sad, he's bouncing off walls and jumping up and down and down and up, spitting emotions out like spoiled milk.

A few days ago, I caught him during one of the sadder moments. Some of the people on the corner were quiet while others vented about how racist the Baltimore police department is, and GD slugged the street lamp like he was training for a prizefight.

"Yo them bitch ass cops! Scared ass cowards," he bawled, kicking the same pole he'd been banging. "Freddie Black is gone. Man, he was a good dude!"

His sister and I walked over to console him, and he slang elbows at us, fell to his knees, and asked God why.

" F reddie Black" is what GD and some of his other friends called him. His real name was Freddie Gray. Gray, 25, was minding his business near Baltimore's Gilmor Homes projects when the cops tried to stop him for no apparent reason. He ran, like a lot of black men do when we see cops, because for our generation, police officers have been the most consistent terrorists in our neighborhoods. Plus, we are currently in a culture where a cop can shoot you if you put hands up, or if you follow their directions, or if you lie down, or if you are asleep. I swear they see black skin and think bull's-eye.

A pack of BCPD officers pursued Gray in traditional bully fashion, caught him, found a legal pocketknife, and arrested him for no reason. Who knew that running with a pocketknife is against the law in Baltimore? Once they got Gray into the van, he seems to have been taken on what we call a Nickel Ride, which is basically when cops rough you up, throw you in a van, and then drive crazy so your body bangs around the back of the vehicle like a pinball, until you reach the police station.

The cops who arrested Gray apparently took it to another level, severing his spinal cord and smashing his voice box. Police officers are responsible for following the rules provided by the Red Cross or National Institutes of Health: Do not bend, twist, or lift the person's head or body, do not attempt to move the person before medical help arrives unless it is absolutely necessary, and do not remove any clothing if a spinal injury is suspected. Instead, these officers handled Gray's nearly lifeless body like a sack of dirty laundry, probably causing further damage to his spinal column.

Gray died in the hospital days later. Now it's national news, and protests are popping up all over the city. Mobs of people, sick of hearing stories over and over again about innocent kids like Gray being murdered.

America is in a state of emergency. I'm not sure why I don't see the president setting our terrorist level at bright orange, because the story of a cop killing an innocent black person surfaces every week. It's important that we use the term "innocent" when describing these victims because in America, you are innocent until proven guilty, and these slain African Americans aren't getting their day in court. There's so many cop killings in the news right now that I'd be surprised if any black person stopped on command. The black bodies are piling up, and I can't even keep up with the names anymore.

Lately I've been having that "cop talk" a couple times a week with my nieces, nephews, or with young people at high schools and middle schools. The convo goes the same way every time. I start out by saying, "Your lives matter. I swear to God they do!" I have to reiterate this as much as possible, because society is telling a different story.

Then I tell them I know every time they check the news or log on to Twitter or Instagram or Facebook or WorldStar, they are seeing people who look just like them being gunned down as if they aren't human by police officers—and many times, those officers get away. But despite that, I insist, you *do* matter. The fact that other videos surface from around the country of white officers trying their best to not shoot dangerous and heavily armed white men weakens my claim. But still I tell them that they matter, even though our legal system tells them otherwise.

I tell them they are human, and the problem is that many of these violent officers don't understand that. They are part of a long history of Americans who don't see value in African and African American life, going all the way back to the days of slavery when it was legal to treat blacks as subhuman. Back when our own American legal system formally identified black people as being three-fifths of a human.

I tell them most of these officers who are committing these murders are scared, racist, and ignorant, so it's up to you to understand, because those cops will never understand or care about you. I tell them to master your perspective and understand what cops are thinking when they see you—because your life could depend on it. The consequence of not understanding police officers is death.

And then I leave them with some rules to follow, things we as black people need to know when being stopped by cops or when dealing with law enforcement in general.

Rules for Survival:

1) Police officers are like mice (*armed* mice)—they are more scared of you than you are of them, so don't startle, or they will shoot. Things that startle them include speaking loudly, being black, moving your hands, and running. If you move your hands or run, they could kill you.

2) Answer their questions in a clear manner. Expressing anger scares them and could lead to your death. Remind them that you are a person; sometimes they forget or were never taught that black people are human. Tell them that you don't have weapons and assure them that they are safe. When police officers don't feel safe around black people, they shoot.

3) Remember that most of the police officers in your neighborhood aren't heroes. They aren't in your neighborhood to protect you but to enforce laws. They don't become cops to save black neighborhoods. They become cops for the salary—which comes with a nice retirement and benefits package. Or because their dads and uncles were cops, and they had no other options. Or because they like the uniform and the guns and the swagger that the whole

cop package gives them. Real heroes care about you. They invest time and energy in your well-being. Cops in black neighborhoods don't.

4) Never think a cop won't shoot you. Your blackness makes you a target to them, and, in many cases, it doesn't matter if you are guilty or innocent.

I close by telling them I know it's hard to remember these rules when you are an innocent person with a gun jammed in your face, but maybe, before it's too late—they'll finally see you as a human. If cops come to believe that you are human, then they won't be so quick to shoot. I have to believe this. Even if it's not true.

In Baltimore, We're All Freddie Gray

When the uprising started in Baltimore in April 2015, it all seemed to be about Freddie Gray, the 25-year-old black man who was viciously attacked by police officers more or less because he looked at them. They subdued him; his spine was nearly severed, his voice box was smashed, and he was hauled off in a police van, even after he requested medical attention multiple times. He died a week later as a result.

But it wasn't only about Freddie Gray. Like him, I grew up in Baltimore, and I, and everyone I know, have similar stories, even if they happened to end a little differently. To us, the Baltimore Police Department is a group of terrorists, funded by our tax dollars, who beat on people in our community daily, almost never having to explain or pay for their actions. It's gotten to the point that we don't call cops unless we need a police report for an insurance claim.

And it's about more than just the cops. We watched as Mayor Stephanie Rawlings-Blake, in conjunction with Police Commissioner Anthony W. Batts, spent over a week investigating what appeared to be an open-and-shut case. I'd like to think that if I broke a person's neck for no reason, I'd be charged in minutes. But the system—even when it's run by a black mayor and a black commissioner, even when a majority of the city council is black—protects the police, no matter how blatant and brutal they are.

I can easily skip right past the cases of innocent victims of police brutality who received a combined amount of nearly $6 million in settlements from the city over the last three years, or Tyrone West, Anthony Anderson, Freddie Gray, and the more than one hundred people killed by local police officers in the last decade, and dive straight into some of the random experiences I've had with cops because I'm black in Baltimore.

When I was ten, a group of thugs kicked in the door to my home, knocking it off the hinges, looking for drugs. They held my family and me at gunpoint for hours while they tore our house apart. When they left, my mom called the cops; they arrived two hours later, treating us as if we were the crooks and complaining about writing the police reports.

When I was twelve, I would play full-court basketball at Ellwood Park, on the city's eastside. One day, the cops came through, saying they were looking for a robbery suspect. Suddenly, about six officers entered the court from all four directions and made everyone lie on the ground, face down. A friend of mine, whom we called Fat Kevin, asked, "Why y'all treatin' us like animals?" One of the cops shouted, "Because you are worthless!" though he also used a much more vulgar, and around here a much more common, term.

Then, when I was fourteen, a cop clotheslined a kid named Rick off a moped. Rick hopped up, yelling, "What did I do?" and was instantly clubbed down by the cop and his partner. Rick's face was badly bruised for weeks.

I can throw in stories from the years in between, or the years after, ranging from pre-K to graduate school. And whether they were marching, or torching a cop car, or cleaning up Tuesday morning, black Baltimoreans have almost all had similar stories.

The police officers in Baltimore, as in many places in the country with dense black populations, are out of control and have been out of control. One of the major reasons is that many Baltimore police officers don't live in Baltimore City; some don't even live in Maryland. Many don't know or care about the citizens of the communities they police, which is why they can come in, beat us, and kill us without a sign of grief or empathy.

Many other Baltimoreans feel the same way, which is why a diverse collection of protesters took to the streets day after day following Freddie Gray's death on April 19. Most of the protests were peaceful. The first acts of violence didn't occur until after a nonviolent, if agitated, protest Saturday night at City Hall. From there, a group of protesters, including me, marched to Camden Yards, where the Baltimore Orioles were playing the Boston Red Sox. As we passed a strip of bars, a group of white baseball fans, wearing both Baltimore and Boston gear, were standing outside yelling, "We don't care! We don't care!" Some called us monkeys and apes. A fight broke out, and people were hurt.

After that, it didn't take much. Some people might ask, "Why Baltimore?" But the real question is, "Why did it take so long?"

The young uprisers of Baltimore have been paying attention to the peaceful protests in Sanford, Florida, Ferguson, Missouri, and New York, only to be let down by the end result over and over again. We are all starting to believe that holding hands, following pastors, and peaceful protests are pointless. The only option is to rise up and force Mayor Rawlings-Blake to make what should be an easy choice: Stop protecting the livelihoods of the cops who killed Freddie Gray, or watch Baltimore burn to the ground.

Missing Black Men

Twenty-five-year-old Freddie Gray was minding his business over at Gilmor Homes—a small low-rise housing project in west Baltimore—when a pack of bloodthirsty predatory cops spotted him, decided to boost their arrest records, and ran him down. I say boost their arrest records because the arresting officers never gave a reason for pursuing or taking him into custody other than stating that they made eye contact with Gray.

Once the cops caught him, they broke his spinal cord, smashed his voice box, and dragged his limp body like a rag doll, breaking every basic rule on handling victims that they should've learned in police academy. Freddie Gray—who was known to his family and friends as a generous jokester who always made sure everybody around him had a great time—died in the hospital a few days later.

Gray's now a part of the list that includes Walter Scott, Justus Howell, Philip White, Eric Harris, and a host of other innocent unarmed black men—all murdered by police officers in a one-month span.

As a black man, I wonder if I'm next. Cops are always eyeing me, pulling me over for nothing, and power tripping when we cross paths. A cocktail of fear, anger, and rage engulfs me, challenging me to match their level of ignorance, but I don't. I remain cool because

I don't want to make that list of unarmed victims or the much more extended list of missing black men in America.

The other day I read a *New York Times* article that said America has 1.5 million missing black men—nineteen thousand alone in my hometown of Baltimore. It blew my mind at first until I sat back and thought about all of the brothers I've lost in my own life—men gunned down in their prime, thrown in jail, reduced to a hazardous life on the streets. Some of the luckier ones get into the military, where they at least have air power to back them up when they exchange gunfire with total strangers. The easiest thing to do in this country as a black man is to be arrested or die or both.

This dude John, a thin, bookish white guy in a patched cardigan, walked up on me in a coffee shop the other day, his palms trembling as he took deep breaths. "Man, what's wrong with you?" I asked, looking over my laptop.

"Dude," he said, "My uncle died, and it's freaking me all the way out; I've never been to a funeral before. I've never seen a dead body—I'm so nervous."

"How old are you again?"

He said that he was forty-two. Being forty-two and never having attended a funeral sounded alien to me. Especially since I saw my uncle's friend murdered when I was five and have been attending funerals ever since. As a result of systemic racism, east Baltimore, like many other dense black populations in America, is full of murder. The bulk of my relatives and black friends have "RIP [Insert fallen solider here]" in their social media bios. Everybody around me has lost somebody.

The *Times* article explained how high incarceration rates and the brutal street culture take a heavy toll on America's black male population. But many other black brothers are dying from simple health issues like having a poor diet, insufficient exercise, and inadequate medical care.

About two months ago, my cousin, Corey Artis, staggered into Johns Hopkins Hospital clenching his chest, thinking he had the flu. There he suffered a massive heart attack and fell into a coma, dying a month later. He was only forty-five years old.

Johns Hopkins Hospital is full of young black men who are plugged up to all types of dialysis machines, liver pumps, spaceship monitors, life-supporting devices, and the rest of the tools needed to aid the countless amount of stroke, heart attack, kidney failure, and high blood pressure/hypertension victims that load their ER daily. The deadly combination of soul food, malt liquor, and our ignorance about their effects is the culprit. When you factor in this grim health reality, I'm left with the feeling that the reported 1.5 million number will only grow.

A week after the Gray murder, I attended one of the many rallies that were being held citywide. A diverse collection of people flooded the lawn of City Hall; even John the patched cardigan guy made it out. In the mix were a collage of relatives—black men I haven't seen in ten-plus years, black men I saw yesterday, and brothers I've never seen in my life. Some were in suits, some covered in tats, some with tatted tears, some with real tears, some with their sons propped high on their shoulders, a few in burger uniforms, and others out slanging bean pies, waters, or #BlackLivesMatter T-shirts.

We were all mourning, weeping, and some began chanting, "Freddie! Fred-die!" I joined in with the bunch of old and new friends in unison and chanted in solidarity.

All of us screaming Freddie's name made the damp and cloudy day less dark. It gave me and many others a moment to rejoice in one of our darkest hours. Our shared strength and anger felt good, at least for that one moment. We knew that justice for Gray wasn't guaranteed—even us coming together again in righteous protest was not a sure thing. As a matter of fact, the only absolute certainty that we "Freddie!"-chanting black men could count on was that a number of us wouldn't make it to the next innocent-black-male-victim rally. Because some of us will join the ranks of the missing.

RIP Freddie.

The Black Crisis Clergy

The black crisis clergy corps are back again. They swept into Baltimore after the death of Freddie Gray with the same ol' custom suits and pulpit oratory that they have used on their macabre death tours since I was a kid.

For years, the same self-appointed black leaders have visited every city mourning yet another black man killed by the police. They swoop in, give a speech, maybe march a mile or two, take some viral social media pictures, and then move on to the next national black tragedy.

Baltimore is only the latest suffering city to witness this circus. Celebrity preachers like Jamal Bryant and Jessie Jackson addressed residents at Freddie Gray's funeral over at New Shiloh Baptist Church in west Baltimore. Some in the city were inspired by their Christian rants and positive agendas. Listeners of a popular Baltimore radio show where I often contribute called in to say how grateful they were for the clergymen's attendance and the peaceful marches they have been fronting.

The old Christian rhetoric seems to work great for the thirty-five-and-over crowd, but it's evident that the young people of Baltimore don't care, feeling that these methods are dated and do not work. In the past, these quick drop-ins by camera-loving holy men from above were good enough for black residents who felt neglected. Not anymore.

Frustrated at how the Gray case is being handled, groups of high school students along with some early twenty-somethings, clicked up with masks and bandanas, rampaged through the streets of Baltimore on the night of Gray's funeral. They trashed stores, flipped cops, and jacked reporters.

During the twenty-four-hour news coverage, the young people involved in this uprising were labeled "thugs." *Thugs?* When white hockey fans win or lose the Stanley Cup and react in the same way, they are called "vandals"—a much less loaded word, even though the hockey hooligans have less social motivation for their rampages. But African Americans angrily reacting to yet one more murder of an innocent community member are instantly called thugs and criminals for similar behavior.

Those kids don't deserve that label. They are simply fed up with all the chronic racism and abuse—and with the Ol' Time Religion protest rituals of the past. They are bored by the sermons and clergy-led marches that lead to nowhere but more of the same. Time after time they see white cops and white freelance enforcers like George Zimmerman get away with murder. If the justice system won't work, these black youths finally concluded, then it's time to go outside the system. Police departments have used violence against the black community for years. These young people are just returning the pain that has been routinely doled out to them in the past.

Meanwhile, black politicians also don't seem to get it, coming across more as scolding parents than as leaders who feel the torment of their people. Mayor Stephanie Rawlings-Blake and President Obama were quick to criticize the actions of Baltimore's young protestors, even resorting to the same racially loaded language ("thugs . . . criminals") heard on Fox News. Yet it took the Baltimore youth rising up to make us all understand that the methods of the past are as broken as a housing project elevator.

I'm not an advocate for violence, but I do commend the young people of Baltimore for their courageous quest for racial equality. They risked their lives in the name of justice for Freddie Gray and showed us that we have to fight for the change we'd all like to see. Now the whole world is applauding the so-called Baltimore Model, which means taking it to the streets and not letting up the pressure until the system finally bends itself in the arc of justice. In Baltimore, we swung hard and first and forced our elected officials to make the right choice.

Our honorable African American political leaders and clergy can learn an important lesson from Baltimore. It's so clear that it might as well be spray-painted on the walls and buses: Lead, follow, or get the hell out of the way.

Smells Like Victory—But the Baltimore Uprise Is Only the Beginning

My Instagram feed has been flooding with pictures of Baltimore City State's Attorney Marilyn Mosby—championing her, crowning her Baltimore's new mayor. In one effortless move, Mosby threw the ball between her legs, whipped it behind her back, splitting a trio of defenders before powering deep in the paint and slam-dunking charges on all six of the cops involved in the death of twenty-five-year-old unarmed Baltimore native Freddie Gray—making history and healing the city at the same time.

Meanwhile, Baltimore has been flooding with happiness and tears of joy. Atheists praised Jesus, homophobes hugged drag queens. The city was like Woodstock, every race marching up and down every major road together, as celebrations erupted across town.

My cousin Mike balanced himself acrobatically on his blue CR 85 motocross bike as he jetted up and down Ashland Avenue in honor of Mosby. Other dirt bikers followed in traditional Baltimore fashion with tricks that excited kids and blocked traffic. I cheered them on, with a foot-long grin, a smile so big it hurt, the first time I smiled in a week.

"We did it, yo! We got them cop bitches, they goin' down!" a kid yelled, guzzling a Pepsi.

My cousin followed, "Fuck yeah! We got 'em! We really got 'em!"

I sat out there with the young dudes for a while, soaking up their positive energy before we all rushed home because of Mayor Rawlings-Blake's 10 o'clock curfew.

On the way home, I thought about the smiling faces I'd seen out all day, along with the mass celebrations, marches, and street performances. A huge number of us African Americans in Baltimore— and probably in most of America—can't say we know what justice is, how justice works, or what justice feels like. I was starting to worry: Would we find out this time?

Last Monday, Baltimore burned—mentally, emotionally, and literally. Freddie Gray lay peacefully in his white casket as the city watched, feeling broken and helpless. Frustrated with the way these stories normally turn out, and with the Baltimore city police department in general, a collection of young people, including me, took to the streets. What started as peaceful meet-ups and protests quickly escalated to what will forever be known as the Baltimore Uprise.

I watched police cars get smashed like aluminum cans and businesses be ripped apart into gutted frames—partially because of Gray but also because of Baltimore's history with the police department. Almost every black person I know from a poor neighborhood can give you a collection of nightmare stories about the BCPD, ranging from their psycho power trips and unnecessary beatings to the way they plant drugs on whom they want to arrest and ruin the lives of sometimes innocent people whenever they see fit. The people of

Baltimore were tired of police brutality being normal, so they took a page from the cops who gather joy from harassing us and decided to strike back just as hard.

I believe, along with many other people, that the destruction was key in Mosby's quick decision to bring about charges, but whatever the case may be, the young state's attorney made the city proud and sparked nationwide celebrations. I just hope we didn't proclaim victory too soon.

Year after year, case after case, and murder after murder, black Americans have sat in pain, forced to watch the killers get off on technicalities. George Zimmerman in Florida had "stand your ground," Darren Wilson in Ferguson had a magical grand jury exempting him of accountability, and I don't even think God knows how the group of New York cops who killed Eric Garner on film with an illegal chokehold got off. Either way, the collection of these cases and many more have created a *These Guys Always Get Away* type of culture, making many of us think killing black people is legal. This explains the current mood in Baltimore.

We are so used to being railroaded by the legal system that dangling a bit of justice in front of us is enough to blindly make us feel like we are equal, when we still have so much work to do. I walked back from the weekend parties with all this on my mind. Once I reached the crib, I called my cousin.

"What up?" he answered.

I told him that celebrating the charges was cool; however, we still did not receive justice for Freddie Gray and the thousands of other victims of police brutality. "It's almost impossible to convict a cop in America," I said, thinking about the laundry list of police officers who beat cases as fast as Ali in his prime.

"How cops be winning all the time?" he asked.

"Well, in Baltimore and many other places in America, you have to register to vote in order to sit on a jury. So many of us don't vote because we've been through the system or don't trust it, meaning that these cops could get a jury full of cop lovers who could care less about our community."

"Yeah, but we got the people on our side this time!" he replied, probably thinking about the multicolored protest. I had to school him on Rodney King and how the officers who beat him on film were able to win their initial case by moving it outside of Los Angeles, where the crime happened, to Simi Valley, a cop-friendly suburb full of jurors who saw nothing wrong with almost beating a black man to death during a traffic stop. Just like Freddie Gray, the Rodney King case was over-saturated with media coverage, and the courts felt King's beaters wouldn't receive a fair case. I'm pretty sure they are going to attempt to do the same thing with these officers.

"I still feel like this won't happen to us!"

He could be wrong, though. Before we hung up, I told him to get out there and spread the word about how important it is to register to vote. Afterward, I sent him a clip of the cops' lawyer, Michael Davey, who said his clients did nothing wrong, with a caption that read, "Yo, this is the pure evil that we are up against."

According to Davey, the officers "at all times acted reasonably and in accordance with their training." His speech made me nauseated, wanting to stop all of the celebrations completely. Achieving justice for Freddie Gray and the rest of the victims of senseless acts of police brutality is going to take more than what we've done to reach this point. Raising awareness and mass voter registration is a start, but how do we change Davey and people with the same mentality?

I'd personally like to start that conversation by asking Davey what if Freddie Gray were his son, his oldest son—the namesake, Michael Davey Jr.? Then I'd ask what if a pack a of rogue police officers stopped young Michael Jr. in his neighborhood for no reason before attacking him and then leaving him limp and breathless in the back of a van with a broken spinal cord and smashed voice box? What if you heard that Michael Jr. asked for medical attention, not one, not two, but three times and was ignored? What if that medical attention could have saved Michael Davey Jr.'s life, and it haunts you as you lay his dead body to rest?

And then, what if you flick on the TV and hear Sean Hannity drag your son's name through the dirt by calling him—the late kid you love—a common criminal and a thug with traces of weed or heroin in his system, even though the cops offered no real reason for stopping your son?

And then I'd pose the same question to the judge, the jury, the cops who did it, and everyone else who thinks like Davey. What if he were *your* son?

Postscript: *It smelled like victory, but it wasn't. None of the cops were convicted. They murdered Freddie Gray and are all free. Freddie Gray did not receive justice.*

O-Ate-Obama

Scores of "Come Celebrate the Victory of Obama!" fliers clogged my inboxes and every social media app I subscribed to back in '08. They sparkled with images of Barack, Michelle, and their Colgate grins. Some had images of Obama stepping on McCain, and others with Barack's head Photoshopped on Mt. Rushmore draped over a Ciroc logo. We made it.

We all felt like we had fought our way through the most highly anticipated and well-documented election in our nation's history—and we actually won. With the exception of Ben Carson and Herman Cain, you'd be hard pressed to find a black person anywhere in America without an Obama T-shirt, hat, hoodie, key chain, bumper sticker, or something!

Getting excited about that '08 election was a first in a year of firsts for many of us. I was one of those twenty-something undergrads who wore the O shirts; I had about ten of them in every flavor with matching bumper stickers and baseball caps; I even donated to the campaign. I learned more about our government and party politics that year than in all of the time I spent in college and grade school combined—and I wasn't alone. Even dope fiends yelled, "Hillary need to get her tired-funky ass out the race!" And dopeboys who traded in their gold chains and sweat suits for Obama-like khakis and button-ups were on the corner fussing over who got the most super delegates. What the fuck are super delegates? Are they bigger than regular delegates? Are they delegates who work out? I'd never heard of super delegates before 2008, and they've seemed to disappear again along with that same Obama magic that drove us crazy.

That Obama magic had people from all around the globe proudly singing his praises. I wouldn't be surprised if a few Klan members secretly wore Obama T-shirts under their robes and checked his name at the ballot box, and why not? That '08 Obama was funny, super cool, beyond brilliant—he played basketball, had a beautiful wife along with two lovely daughters whom he promised to give a dog if he were to win, and was basically everything Grandma wants you to grow up to be, packed into one fit dude who never came off as arrogant, disingenuous, or disgustingly elite. His grassroots campaign made him revolutionarily accessible through social media. He included all of us disenfranchised-feeling black people in the political process by teaching us how and why our government was failing us and what needed to be done to bring about "real change." Obama identified the core hopes and shortcomings that poor African Americans and poor whites share while remaining savvy enough to inspire the well off. He walked unwalkable lines, smoothly bringing together classes, ethnicities, and genders of people who traditionally had oil-and-water-like histories—rightfully putting him in the White House and the party fliers in my inbox.

Fast forward to 2015, and you'd be hard pressed to find a black person in America anywhere with an Obama T-shirt, hat, hoodie, key chain, bumper sticker, or something! That Obama magic deflated just like Al—Roker or Sharpton. Liberals felt defeated as the Obama administration carried out the same Bush-like war tactics and even went on to hurl more drones and arrest more whistleblowers than W. Meanwhile, African Americans lost steam as we watched historic job creation across the board while our unemployment rate continued in the wrong direction, even getting higher than pre-recession levels. And, of course, the Republicans never liked him because he's black—and because even though he took care of their friends on Wall Street and in the Pentagon, he's in the wrong party. Obama could propose that the federal government grant $10 million checks to every white person in America, and Boehner, Rush, Hannity, along with the rest of those delusional Fox mascots, would still hate his guts. I expected that knee-jerk Obama bashing from the right— but who knew that the man who inspired so much joy in '08 would get it from the center and left, too?

I still can't help but think that Obama's heart is in the right place. He put forth so many policies, initiatives, and programs with the purpose of providing an equal playing field for minorities—programs that range from job creation and mentorship to actually giving more money to historically black colleges and universities. But any- and everything he proposed, regardless of who could benefit, has been met with resistance by almost every Republican in Congress—not to mention the screaming Tea Party hordes in the streets.

As for the pro-Obama camp, we were naive to view President Obama as our black savior. Hope can be inspiring, and we all need more of it—but it was never realistic to think that his eight years in the White House could erase five-hundred-plus years of structural racism. Just the same way, it would be foolish to think that if Hillary wins in 2016, the battle for women's rights will end. Will women no longer be sexualized in the workplace or assaulted on campus? Will they receive the equal pay and get the universal respect that they deserve? Don't hold your breath. Nonetheless, the idea of a woman president—just like a black president—is a small step in the right direction.

All in all, I still feel like Obama did everything he could within his limited powers and under the political circumstances—except to carry out his role as a teacher, which is probably extra difficult because despite what Republicans think, he isn't just president of African Americans, but president of the United States, and maintaining that balance is probably like playing Jenga drunk in the dark. However, these teachable moments are what made President Obama's '08 campaign so successful. As a candidate, he taught us how to be active and why we need to get out and vote. In other words, he taught us how to win. But as president, he's failed to shed light on the systemic racism that prohibited a huge part of "the real change" he preached about, that change we all wanted to see. His passionate sermon on behalf of the slain Reverend Clemente Pinckney at the memorial service in Charleston in June 2015 showed how Obama can hit those heights as the Educator-in-Chief about race when he wants to, similar to the Obama who gave that amazing speech on race in 2008—we can only hope that he'll use this final year in office to keep enlightening the nation.

What our country really needs came to me the other day in New York. I walked out of my hotel room in midtown to three eager, smiley cab drivers out front. To my surprise, they were polite, asking me if I needed a ride, inviting me into their cars. I was confused, I hadn't been to New York in a while, but I remember how hard it was to get a cab during my last visit. Hundreds of cabbies with empty back seats would drive right by me—I felt that diving in front of their moving cars wouldn't even make them stop. But now they are offering red carpet service as I respectfully declined and hopped in my Uber.

Yes, it was the image of a black man in the White House that maybe has made it a little easier for us to make our way through the day, or at least to get a ride. But Uber has probably changed the racial dynamic in the cab industry more than Obama has. Because of Uber, cabs can't *afford* to discriminate against me any longer. The cab industry had no choice but to change.

America needs a game-changing Uber shift in the political arena—a massive influx of minority activists, politicians, educators, and history makers. One black man cannot bring about that change, but an army of people committed to making opportunity available for everybody can and will.

BONUS TRACKS

Make America Hate Again

Pay close attention to Donald Trump's little Mussolini imitations, his messaging to the KKK and neo-Nazi crowd that he barely makes an effort to conceal, the blunt ways that he has peaceful African-American students removed from events time and time again . . . and you'll see that Donald Trump's "Make America Great Again" slogan means completely removing black Americans from the narrative of this country. One black protester in Fayetteville, North Carolina was socked in the face and Trump cheered on the old coward who sneaked in the lucky punch. When the video went viral and the assaulter was charged, Trump hopped on *Meet the Press* and said, "I'll have people looking in to paying his legal fees." Who would think that a person could run a successful campaign centered on such blatant racism in 2016?

I'd file Trump's campaign with the hottest, most trashiest, substance-free crap that has dominated pop culture over the last ten years. It's a *Real House Wives*-type reality show—his ravings are as enlightening as a Kardashian family squabble mixed with Honey Boo Boo's diet tips, and yet, people are listening to him. People are proudly wearing "Make America Great Again" T-shirts that were made in Mexico and filling arenas to listen to him. The only thing worse than his half-baked ideas, the boasts about his up-and-down business career, the inflated claims about his body parts, his pouting, preening, bubbled face, and his general snarkiness are his rallies.

Trump rallies are sad. Really sad. Even sadder than the Sarah Palin rallies back in 2008. Every inch of the screen is full of haters, a diverse collection of enraged whiteness, their skin tones ranging from peach-pink to Trump-red. Some are in suits and awkward snap backs while other wear cowboy hats, suspenders, soiled T-shirts, and denim—but they're all bound by a common fury. These people are white and they live in America so I've yet to figure out why they are so mad, but their discontent is on full display as they scream, fuss and chant all the way up until the moment that The Donald commands the podium. Then, after the cheers subside, Trump whips them into an even hotter frenzy, yelling about a Mexican wall to be built by Mexicans, the grim fate that awaits Muslim militants and their families, his piles and piles of money, his penis size, his big poll numbers and how America will be great again. Billowing clouds of hot air, and an endless stream of playground taunts, putdowns and boasts that a sixth-grader would be too embarrassed to make.

The poor and forgotten white people who rush to Trump rallies need a serious reality check. So let me take a crack at it. Number one, dear Trump supporter, Donald can't relate to you. He doesn't eat the food that's killing you, take the medicine they try out on you, or truly understand your hardships. He doesn't even have an honorable American story. He was born into money and never worked a hard day in his life. Check his smooth, small, clean manicured hands. Unlike you, he's been allowed to fail over and over again—to bankrupt a countless number of businesses and to defraud investors and consumers—because of his name, his connections and his clout. Most of you can't afford to stay in his trash hotels or buy his over-overpriced condos. Despite your skin color, Trump fan, you probably have more in common with the minorities you're demonizing than the candidate you're cheering.

Number two, do you really want an America without black people? Come on, we all know that America would not be America without black people. Forget how this country rose to power through free labor (meaning slavery), or how blacks were used as guinea pigs in experiments that led to many of the advancements in modern medicine, or how most of the people who attend Trump rallies probably run home on the weekends to watch their favorite Negroes score touchdowns and dunk basketballs. Seriously, you really don't want blacks in America? There's no Elvis, Beatles, or Beach Boys without black music. Then there's the traffic light, potato chips, the gas mask, the mailbox, the blood bank, the carbon filament for light bulbs, the pacemaker control unit, the fire proof safe, the telegraph, the home video game console, the imaging X-Ray spectrometer, mobile refrigeration, the elevator, the mop, the almanac, the car phone, ice cream, the lawn mower, the fire extinguisher, the ironing board, and air conditioning units--all of which wouldn't exist without African Americans. The list goes on and on and on.

This country would be a shell of itself without black and brown people. We aren't taking your jobs—many of us are frustrated and unemployed too. It's the greedy Trump-type plutocrats—and hell, even Trump himself—who are responsible for outsourcing opportunity to foreign countries for profit.

This is the bitter truth, Trump worshipper. Your political hero has contempt for you. He doesn't give a damn about you. To him you're the lowest, most demeaning word he can think of. You're a loser. And if you actually vote for him in November, you'll be the biggest loser of all.

The Next Freddie Gray

"Hey Mr. Watkins, thank you so much for coming out," said a twenty-something-year-old white woman in dark frames and an Urban Outfitters-looking flannel, after I finished talking to a crowd in the Pacific Northwest. "I'm just a white woman from Seattle. I'm a photographer, and I don't really understand all of these black issues but I want to help. Like, how can I make a difference?" She then shrugged and went on to say that she took amazing photos of the protests in Ferguson, Missouri.

"You aren't powerless," I told her. "Instead of just taking photos of suffering people, pull one of them aside and teach them how to use your camera. Tell them what a DSLR is, and about aperture and f-stops. Expose them to something they never heard of before. Tell them that being an artist is a career option, and then you will be making a difference." Heavy head nods and applause followed.

Activism and writing has taken me to many cities, and I'm always confronted with that question—not just from white people, but suburban blacks, hip liberal Asians and the racially ambiguous. It doesn't matter what you look like or where you come from, everyone can skill share. Skill sharing is key in pulling us away from the muck of class and racial divides in our cities, including police violence and black-on-black crime.

Leaders, elected officials and people who care in general need to think about these solutions as American justice is put on trial in the Freddie Gray case—and in countless other courtrooms across the country. What skills and opportunities did Gray have before he was grabbed by police and thrown into the back of the van where he died?

I'm sick of people showing up to the party late. Famous preachers, corny musicians and politicians popping up every time a black kid gets shot. The real question is, could Freddie Gray have called you if he needed a job reference or some life advice? Of course the whole world wants justice for Freddie now, but the world wasn't worried about giving him a fair shake when he was alive and trying to make it like the rest of us. The same goes for Mike Brown in Ferguson. Could Brown have reached out to you if he needed help finding scholarships to pay his college tuition? Would you have shaken Trayvon Martin's hand, or stopped to give him directions if he was lost? Really, would you? Because I know royal activists who don't touch people. We all need to move beyond the easy rhetoric and the short-lived displays of support for victims. We need to find creative and ongoing ways to unite.

We must try our best to make ourselves available and helpful. What's more valuable than a mentor you can call or visit when you need a hand? Conservatives—and, truly, *all* those who are fearful and ignorant about black people—get this all twisted when these opportunity conversations come up. Black people don't want handouts—just in case you forgot, our ancestors built this country through brutal and harsh slave labor—we want a fair shake like everyone else. I'll never expect a level playing field in this country; however, if you really care and want to do something like that woman from Seattle, please be a mentor to somebody in need. Share your skills, your knowledge, your connections. Pass along some of the wisdom that got you to where you are today.

In America, Everybody Sees Color

"You're that teacher from CNN that hates cops!" laughed a pudgy white guy in a folded Ravens hat. He was three chairs down and slid one closer. We were in an almost empty bar at Hartsfield-Jackson airport, in Atlanta, both heading back to Baltimore.

"I'm a cop in Baltimore County and have been for ten years, what's your name?" He asked, as he signaled the bartender.

"I'm D. Watkins, man," I said, extending my hand for a hand-shake. "I don't hate all cops, but some of ya'll, *mannnn* . . . Never mind." I'm definitely switching topics. I had a long four days—six book-tour stops, back-to-back, talking about cops and shootings and black-on-black crime and systemic racism and gun laws and on and on and on.

The bartender dropped off his beer, and switched the TV to ESPN.

"I don't really know what's going on in Baltimore City," the cop said, inhaling his beer. "I know they needed us to help out when those crazy riots kicked off. Baltimore City always needs help. What do think is going to happen with the Gray case?"

"I don't know, what do you think is going to happen with the Ravens? I'm sick of losing," I answered. He dove into his life story.

His award-winning kids, his nice home, his years of service, his wife, his vision.

Being a Z-list local celebrity on TV does this; it makes people feel entitled to you. You are not famous enough to be unapproachable, but famous enough to be recognized and therefore responsible for listening to everything everyone says, digesting every narrative—even if you are with your family—and answering every question with engaging solutions that leave them with a sense of fulfillment, the ability to walk away like, "That D. Watkins is a good guy, he is really one of the good ones!" Not today.

I ate my dinner as he rambled. He's conservative but voted for Martin O'Malley, Maryland's former Democratic governor. He kept going and going; it was a verbal marathon, and he was winning by a million lengths. Some people really don't understand how conversations work: You have to let other person get a word in. I'd die if my flight got delayed, I'd pay to leave early.

"D., I don't see color. Never have and never will," he told me. That woke me up. White people always say this, and it's not true, especially not in America. In America, everybody sees color, even the non-racist—we're programmed to generalize and stereotype.

"I gotta call you on that one, man, we all see color. Color is how this country works. If I see a white person, I'm going to think they that they love mayonnaise. And if I see a 90-year-old, one-legged black woman, I'm going assume that she's NBA-ready and can dunk a basketball backwards!"

We all laugh; the bartender laughs the loudest. "I agree with this guy on that one," he says, pointing in my direction. "I'm from the South and came up in a mostly white setting. But I hate mayo!

And my girlfriend's Asian, but I'm way better at math. People put the both of us in boxes all of the time."

"You guys are racist!" laughed the cop. "But seriously, no disrespect. Some of those cops involved with the Gray case were black. How can we say it was race thing?"

I've explained this ten thousand times, one more wouldn't hurt: "You don't have to be a racist to play a key role in perpetuating a racist system. You know there were many black slave catchers back in the day. The problem is that police officers protect and serve the rich and terrorize the poor."

The cop shook his head in emphatic *no-way* motions and got ready to launch. This was clearly getting too real for the bartender, who slid into another conversation. "As a cop, that wouldn't happen on my watch. Look, those officers in Baltimore were screwups, but they aren't murderers. It was an honest mistake. You really don't know how it is until you are out there dealing with dangerous people all of the time."

And that's my main issue with police officers. They do no wrong. They are the ultimate justifiers, always making excuses for each other. It's the only profession where the employees are eager to dismiss murder as if that badge makes one morally exempt.

"Yeah I don't know," I said. "Just like you don't know what it's like to be on my side . . . and we both know that if Gray was white, he'd be alive right now."

"Well, I can't say that. I guess, we'll have to agree to disagree on that one," said the cop. Joe Flacco flashed across the screen. The reporter began to speak about Baltimore's woes, just like we were doing. "D., you think Flacco is overpaid? We paid him too much, right?"

"I don't know man," I said, dumping my cash on the table. I thought about giving him one of my books, with the hope of him reading it and gaining a different perspective, but decided not to— he has a job, so he should buy it, free books are better in the hands of young people who aren't as poisoned by society, tradition and all those things that prohibit growth and the enhancement of social relations. Many of us are stuck in our ways—just like that cop, we water down our own faults, if we even acknowledge them at all.

All this left me with one question. If I'm perfect, you are perfect, the cops are perfect, the community is perfect, and the politicians are perfect—then where do all of these problems come from?

Opportunity Is Mightier Than Guns

Laptops For Guns is a simple program making a big impact in Baltimore. You find a gun, dust it off, hand it over to Digit All Systems, a nonprofit that spreads computer knowledge in the Baltimore inner city, and walk away with a brand new laptop. The exchange is held at the Urban League in West Baltimore and gains more popularity every year, with support from the Mayor Stephanie Rawlings-Blake and a host of other local politicians. To date, Digit All founder and CEO Lance Lucas is responsible for 89 guns being taken off the streets, and he plans on doubling that number this year.

I met Lucas, whose personality towers over his six-feet, three-inch frame, at a conference in Washington, D.C. and rapped with him afterward. We swapped ideas on the negative issues that affect our community, and how we all need to evolve into more solution-based-thinking instead of agenda-less marches. "Laptops For Guns is only the tip of the iceberg!" he told me. "I just use that to get the community interested. If you want the real story, my man, come check my program out when you're back in Baltimore."

I always want the real story, so I hit Lance on the jack about a week later: "Meet me on Rose Street, it's real down there," he said. I know Rose Street. I grew up in that area—it's like the rough section of a rough neighborhood, tricked out with open-air drug markets and uncertainty.

I pulled up behind Lance and jumped out, to a mini-celebration of pounds and hugs from some old friends—a mini-celebration because there have already been over fifty murders in Baltimore this summer and any one of us could be next.

"Yo, this is Rose Street Shelter," said Lucas, pointing to a slim row house on the corner. "My student Trayvon was living here before I got him and his brother A+ certified." A+ is a nationally recognized certificate awarded to people who have the ability to troubleshoot, test, manage, install and solve minor software and hardware issues on computing equipment.

Trayvon Leonard, 23, walked out of the shelter looking like he came from the future in his limited edition Google Frame glasses. He was going on and on about his upcoming trip to New Orleans, where he will eventually be moving for three months to teach an A+ Certification course.

Trayvon had been working with Lucas for four years. Lucas also taught his twin brother, Tracy, at the Baltimore Talent Development High School. The twins fell on hard times shortly after graduation and ended up homeless. They lived on porches and park benches until they found the Rose Street Shelter. "Man we ain't have nothin," Trayvon told me. "I remember Lance had told my brother that if we needed him, [we should] call him—so we did," he added.

Lucas helped the boys find housing and enrolled them in his A+ certification course. From there, they learned basic computer and cellphone repair and instantly started making money. "I didn't know my life would change so fast," said Trayvon. He adjusted the lenses on his Google frames: "Don't get me wrong, you have to work hard, but any- body can do it, as long as they work."

Trayvon and his brother Tracy have gone on to train over five hundred people in A+ classes, with a ninety-five percent certification rate. "That's what it's about, learning these skills and sharing them," said Jason Brooks, one of the few black software engineers at Google, who has served over a decade in prison and has found redemption through technology as well. "I don't have to teach coding at Lance's program, but I do it so that my brothers and sisters can experience success like me," he said.

July 25, the day for the annual Laptops For Guns exchange, rolled around. Lance had made last-minute trips to Best Buy and Hip Hop chicken for extra computers and food, preparing for a massive crowd. His company Digit All funded everything—Lance even bought the computers that were to be given away during the exchange.

A line of eager people formed out front with their pistols and rifle cases, waiting to swap them for a new opportunity. Armed SWAT dudes wrapped the block in full military gear. An eager Lucas popped in and out of the center, greeting cops and gun traders. He was rocking a Street Geek tech tee, a prototype shirt that will be offered by a new line created by him and the Leonard twins.

"They're coming for the laptops, but I'm gonna school them on making more through these certifications," Lance told me before we walked into the center, adding, "I really think we can use technology to end systemic poverty. I have the cure and it's through technology-driven education." Out of one hundred people

from a municipal workforce development program that uses Lucas
to retrain unemployed workers, over sixty percent found jobs and
escaped poverty.

"You do the math," he said.

My Negus

A silly photo of six little ignorant high school girls went viral. They attend Desert Vista high school in Phoenix. It was picture day, and a group of seniors wore black shirts with individual gold letters that spelled out "BEST *YOU'VE *EVER* SEEN* CLASS* OF*2016," when arranged. During the photo session, the six students mentioned slid to the side and begin taking their own pictures. The letters on their shirts spelled out NI**ER.

Someone posted the picture—and a public frenzy soon followed, with testimonies from a diverse collection of offended and upset students. The image continued to circulate all over the world making it to me thirty-plus times—three via text and the rest scattered on social media from various tweeters, ranging from rightfully infuriated black people to retweets from the cowardly troll accounts that champion racism.

M y Apple dictionary app defines nigger as an offensive noun, a contemptuous term for a black or dark-skinned person. It goes on to explain that the word was used as an adjective denoting a black person as early as the 17th century and has long had strong offensive connotations. Today it remains one of the most racially offensive words in the language. Also referred to as "the N-word," it is sometimes used by black people in reference to other black people in a jocular or disparaging manner, or some variant in between.

Apple is only semi-right—primarily because the offense is based solely on who's talking.

Way back when I was six, I was convinced that my cousin Kevin was the best nine-year-old to ever wrap stubby fingers around a bat. He was greater than great, a lefty who slapped any and every type of pitch out of Ellwood Park. When purposely walked, Kevin had that Deion Sanders speed, quick enough to steal every base and slide home.

Those skills earned Kevin a slot on teams all over the city. Often, I'd tag along. On one of those bright days, Kev took care of business as usual, slapping a few homers and snagging a few fly balls. Midway through the game, the pitcher beelined Kev with the ball, allowing him to take first. He stole second and third and then tried to gun for home plate. The catcher waved his mitt in Kev's direction as he slid over the base. The umpire called him out, though it clearly could have gone either way. Kevin and the catcher exchanged words as he headed for the bench. The catcher yelled, "This nigger is always cheating!"

Kevin snapped, spun around and tackled the catcher. From there he lunged a knee on the kid's torso, and whaled on his face until his mask popped off. It took two adults to pull him off. "You'll never play in this league again!" a coach or parent yelled as we exited the park.

"Yo, you good?" I asked, "You went crazy on that fat boy!"

Kev, who called me his "favorite lil nigga" almost every day, stopped and lasered me with intense eyes; a vein throbbed and parted his forehead into quadrants. "D, listen!" he squeezed my small shoulders. "If a white person ever call you a nigger, you better beat their ass, or I will beat your ass!"

From that day on, I knew nigger, nigga, nig, or any of other variation of the term belonged to black people. As years passed, I gave the same speech to my younger siblings, little cousins and all of their friends.

The flip side is that we never really had to apply the rule. See, we're from east Baltimore and never really interacted with whites other than some schoolteachers and housing police. The teachers never called us nigger, and we couldn't whip the white officers who used the word, because they had guns, coupled with a license to kill.

College taught me that the word was originally a 15th- or 16th-century Spanish-Portuguese word meaning black. By the 1800s the term had became a permanent fixture in American language. African slaves and free blacks alike were niggers—bottom feeders, subhuman, the lowest of the low.

Back then, similar to now, blacks were taught to praise whiteness—white religions and gods, white traditions, white ideals. We ourselves adopted the word, and thus it entered our language with the same derogatory meaning, before we redefined and branded it as a term of love, hate, unity, connection, betrayal or whatever else we wanted to use it for. As the term became more and more forbidden to whites, we branded it more and more as our own.

But is this creation myth about the word even true? Is it a word invented by white people with the purpose of identifying and degrading blacks? Any student of history or American culture knows our nation's lust for controlling narratives and pushing perspectives that promote and glorify whiteness.

I never questioned what I learned in school about the origin of the word until I stumbled across a YouTube clip from 2007 of ESPN's national spelling bee. Andrew Lay, a tiny *Home Alone* kid-looking sixth-grader from North Carolina approached the mic. The announcer challenged him to spell "negus." Andrew swallowed his throat, and responded with a blank pause before requesting a repeat along with the definition and origin. Some people in the audience who looked like they were his parents gasped.

"Ethiopian to Amharic," the announcer said. "A king, it's used as the title of the sovereign of Ethiopia."

Andrew froze, bit his lip and asked for a sentence.

"The negus ruled Ethiopia until 1974."

Andrew requested the definition again, blinked and said, "N-e-g-u-s? Negus."

The crowd applauded, confirming his correctness. Andrew fist pumped like Kobe after a game winner while heading back to his seat.

The same dictionary on my Mac defines "negus" as a ruler, or the supreme ruler of Ethiopia. The word's origin dates back to the 14th century, far before n***er, which makes me question who created the word and if there is a connection between its African origin, the Portuguese version and the term that made it into the States.

I never feel offended when a black person calls me nigga or nigger (accent and pronunciation based on the region they represent); however, I'm beyond offended when white people use the word—kind of how a veteran would feel if you pissed on an American flag, and rightfully so. The N-word is *our* word, it's a term only to be used between African Americans—it's a part of our established culture.

There's American culture, and then there are subcultures within American culture that need to be respected. I went to college with students from Asian cultures who told me that direct eye contact could be considered disrespectful. My grandma wanted you to take your hat off once you entered her home; many churches have the same rule. My writing teacher taught us that non-Jewish people calling Jewish people "Jews" could be offensive. I know Habesha families that require you to remove your shoes when you enter their place. The list goes on and on.

The fact is that white people need to get over it. They have no need to use the N-word—they aren't culturally connected to it in a positive way, and it does nothing to enhance their journey, experience or wellbeing. The ones who use the word or flirt with its existence, like the silly girls in the picture, simply want conflict. It's not their word, so they want to control it—they want to cause a stir, offend or be a part of a culture that they can never fully understand. They use it as a trigger word and then run from it when people react in a negative way.

The people who mentor or teach the girls in that stupid photo—and indeed, those who mentor or teach all non-black kids who want to play around with this word—need to do more than explain why their action was culturally insensitive. They need to teach them how rough it can be for women in this country and how they can easily end up in a different sort of nasty photo. Discrimination doesn't discriminate.

What Do You Expect?

Twenty-five-year old Micah Xavier Johnson filled his clips to the tip with the anger, frustration and hate that many African Americans in this country share. Tired of racism, tired of police brutality, and our country's long history of dehumanizing black people—Johnson strapped himself with that hate and canceled the lives of five police officers.

Multiple news agencies reported that the former Army reservist had bigger plans for destruction—a raid of his home turned up more weapons, bomb-making material and journals with detailed plans of action for a later date. Micah never reached that date—his tipping point was the back-to-back murders of two innocent black males, Alton Sterling in Baton Rouge and Philando Castile in Falcon Heights, Minnesota. Both homicides were caught on video and both instantly went viral.

Mostly peaceful protests and demonstrations broke out in cities all across the country, including Dallas, not too far from where Johnson lived. He posted up in a parking garage near the rally, scoped out his enemies and dumped the same hate that officers have been dumping on black people everyday since the beginning of their profession.

The normal media circus followed, with constant press conferences and round-the-clock coverage. The usual talking heads from the Black-Death-Tour were busy explaining race without any real understanding of the topic or actual proximity to black people. As Johnson was identified and the story developed, reporters pegged him as a militant who hated white people, who was fired up about Black Lives Matter, and who went on a cop-killing mission as a result. Some professional mourners from the Black-Death-Tour lingered for awhile on the fringes of the media spotlight; but soon, an influx of crying, hyper-emotional cops took over cable news.

I get it—police officers are sad because they lost some of their fellow brothers. I have empathy, real empathy because I've lost many of my brothers and best friends to senseless acts of violence, and I've seen cops murder black people on camera every week. I truly feel their pain—but how come they never feel ours?

Police officers pop up with the same statements every time they murder an innocent black person:

1) **What about black on black murders?** As if that justifies police murders. Like white on white murder doesn't exist. The U.S. Justice Department's statistics bureau reports that 84 percent of white murder victims are killed by white people. The number for blacks is 94 percent—it's not that big of a difference. America is segregated, and that's the primary reason why people kill people who look like them.

2) **We don't have all the facts.** Cops *never* have all the facts. Eric Garner was murdered in broad daylight, on film, screaming that he could not breathe as the life was squeezed out of him. He was choked to death for no reason by a notoriously

aggressive New York cop for all the world to see. And yet there somehow weren't enough facts to indict.

Likewise, South Carolina cop Michael Slager was also captured on video shooting Walter Scott in the back, in cold blood. Slager committed a flagrant act of murder, and then lied about it, claiming that Scott grabbed for his gun, when he really just ran for his life.

But these shocking videos normally don't matter anyway, because these killer cops are never held accountable for their criminal actions. In fact, the only person involved with the Garner case who was arrested and given a prison sentence was Ramsey Orta, the young man who bravely filmed the killing of Garner. The cops were never going to let Orta get away with that. And the police have subjected the two men who filmed and distributed the Alton Sterling video to the same outrageous harassment.

Unsurprisingly, despite the blatant video evidence, no homicide charges were brought against Slager either. When the feds finally stepped in to charge the killer cop with a lesser, civil rights violation, the media greeted this news as if the angels of justice were singing from heaven above—even though a lot more than Scott's civil rights were violated that day in North Charleston.

3) **They acted within their training.** So your training is to kill unarmed blacks?

Therefore, following Dallas, my question to the law is: what do you expect? The never-ending assault on black lives by cops across the country created Micah Johnson. Did you really think that the constant harassment and act of violence by men in blue—men with badges and a license to kill—would *not* someday produce a Micah Johnson? Would *not* finally drive the victims of this predatory behavior crazy? Like many of us, Johnson knew that our black lives actually *don't* matter in this country.

Look at how blacks are treated in this country. I'm not talking about the cops here, but about the schools, the job market, the prison-industrial complex, the health care system, the food supply. About the way that our black president runs to Dallas to comfort cops but never made it to the grieving streets of Baltimore, which is just down the highway from his home, or to Ferguson or Baton Rouge or Albuquerque or Oakland, or any of the cities where the streets have been soaked with our blood and tears. Police shootings are just business as usual in these American neighborhoods.

No, Black Lives Matter didn't create the rage in Johnson nor did the protest campaign co-sign his actions. That rage comes naturally for black men and women growing up in America. And once that fury begins to sprout within you, it's all too easy in our country to use a gun to give it full expression. There's only one way to address the rage that erupted in Micah Johnson. We need to put the guns down—and that means cops too. Put the guns down and STOP KILLING BLACK PEOPLE.

Acknowledgments

I would like to thank my entire team at Hot Books/Skyhorse Publishing, and all of the talented editors who made these essays come alive in the many places where they previously appeared including *Salon*, *The New York Times*, *The Baltimore Sun*, *Aeon*, *The City Paper*, *1729 mag*, and *The Guardian*.

Praise for *The Beast Side*:

"A blunt, eloquent argument for the forgotten in our cities."
—DAVID SIMON, author of *The Corner* and creator of HBO's *The Wire*

"The twenty-first-century Civil Rights era is upon us, and one of the most compelling new voices to listen to is D. Watkins. *The Beast Side* is a riveting and important read no matter what your preconceived notions are on the state of race relations in America today."
—CHUCK TODD, correspondent on NBC's *Meet the Press*

"D. Watkins is a very sharp young talent who transformed himself from a dealer on the streets to a leading voice of his generation who is determined to see justice for the black community. *The Beast Side* is raw, intelligent, and at times humorous—and a necessary narrative in these challenging times!"
—MICHAEL ERIC DYSON, author of *The Black Presidency: Barack Obama and the Politics of Race in America*

"Our generation is seeking honest, courageous thought leaders and yearning for solutions to this country's seemingly hopeless race problem—D. Watkins is the former and *The Beast Side* offers so much of the latter. It's a necessary read and the perfect bridge for the older and younger generations trying to make a change"
—ISSA RAE, writer and creator of *Awkward Black Girl* and HBO's *Insecure*

"Brilliant. *The Beast Side* is just the latest illustration of why D. Watkins's voice is so important to our community. Understand his words, and let's work to make our community better."
—WES MOORE, *New York Times* bestselling author of *The Work* and *The Other Wes Moore*

"An honest, sobering exploration of blackness in the context of Baltimore and the unrest. And Watkins is a skilled storyteller, giving voice to a range of hard truths."
—DERAY MCKESSON, activist for We the Protestors

D. WATKINS is Editor at Large for Salon.com. His work has been published in the *New York Times*, *Guardian*, *Rolling Stone*, and other publications. He holds a master's in Education from Johns Hopkins University and an MFA in creative writing from the University of Baltimore. He is a college professor at the University of Baltimore and founder of the BMORE Writers Project. Watkins has been the recipient of numerous awards including Ford's Men of Courage and a BME Fellowship. Watkins is from and lives in East Baltimore. He is the author of *The Cook Up: A Crack Rock Memoir* and *The Beast Side: Living (and Dying) While Black in America*.